D1124092

NORTH AMERICAN CHURCHES

FROM CHAPELS TO CATHEDRALS

MARILYN CHIAT, PH.D.

Publications International, Ltd.

Marilyn Chiat holds a Ph.D. in art history and specializes in religious art and architecture. She has written several articles and books on this subject, including *America's Religious Architecture: Sacred Places for Every Community* and *Handbook of Synagogue Architecture*. In addition, she was an expert witness on the Landmark Commission for Chicago and served as a consultant for the Minnesota Historical Society.

Contributing writer: Eric Peterson is a Denver-base freelance writer who has contributed to numerous periodicals, travel guides, and books. His recent credits include *Roadside Americana*, the 5th edition of *Frommer's Montana & Wyoming* and stories for *Arthur Frommer's Budget Travel*, *EnCompass*, and *Westword*.

Louis Weber, CEO
Publications International, Ltd.
7373 North Cicero Avenue
Lincolnwood, Illinois 60712

Manufactured in China.

8 7 6 5 4 3 2 1

ISBN: 1-4127-1020-0

Library of Congress Control Number: 2004104585

CONTENTS

INTRODUCTION
NEW WORLD, NEW RELIGIONS

The psalmist tells us not once but twice to "worship the Lord in the beauty of holiness" (Psalm 29:2; 96:9 KJV). These two verses have had an enormous impact throughout the ages on the appearance of religious architecture, for the word "beauty" can take on many meanings. This was certainly the case in the religious battles that tore apart the Christian church, most notably in the years leading up to the Reformation in the 16th century. Roman Catholics believed their consecrated churches represented God's sacred dwelling and, therefore, embellished them with beautiful art. Protesters, including Martin Luther, argued that the beauty of holiness does not lie in material things but in the people gathered to hear and participate in the spoken Word.

In the midst of this turmoil a new world was discovered—a world perceived by many Europeans as a *tabula rasa,* or a "clean slate," upon which a new chapter in the history of Christianity could be written. *North American Churches: From Chapels to Cathedrals* traces that history as it reveals itself in the houses of worship erected by people who came to this new land with the hopes and dreams of establishing a new and better way of life for themselves and their descendants. Faith is what guided them to these shores, and faith is what kept their dreams alive.

The first Europeans to arrive in the New World can be divided into three major groups: Spanish Catholics seeking gold and converts, Pilgrims and Puritans fleeing religious persecution, and Anglicans seeking new land and markets. They established a pattern that became uniquely American—a diversity of faiths, each with its own interpretation of the beauty of holiness.

By the 17th century, Anglicans were occupying the southern colonies; the Puritans, now known as Congregationalists, controlled Massachusetts and were a presence in other northern colonies; and the Spanish and French were successfully converting native peoples living in the Southwest. Other faiths were also present, as is evident in a letter to the British Board of Trade in 1686 by Edmond Andros, the English governor of New York. Andros expressed bewilderment over the variety of religious groups occupying his colony: "There are religions of all sorts, one Church of England[,] several Presbyterians and Independents, Quakers and Anabaptists of several sects [and] some Jews."

This was but a harbinger of what was to come. Between 1680 and 1760 the colonial population grew from approximately 250,000 to more than 2 million. Each colony established its own rules regarding religion: Roger Williams opened Rhode Island to all faiths, as did William Penn when he established his "Holy Experiment" in Pennsylvania. Massachusetts remained off-limits to all but fellow Congregationalists, while the Church of England became the official church of Virginia, and English Roman Catholics founded Maryland.

Unlike in Europe, conditions in the New World led to religious competition as each group sought to convert the "unchurched." Revivalist fervor among Protestants was fanned by the fear that the lack of a state-sponsored church would result in an "un-Christian" nation. As a result, preachers such as Jonathan Edwards, a Congregationalist, and Henry Melchior Muhlenberg, a German Lutheran, began to electrify crowds with their sermons.

This era, which began in 1734 and lasted until the eve of the Revolutionary War, is known as the First Great Awakening. It was the beginning of what has become a characteristic of American church life—mass evangelicalism. The result was the formation of a number of new Protestant denominations, including the Society of Friends (Quakers), Methodists, Universalists, Unitarians, Shakers, and Free Will Baptists. It was also during this time that America's founders began to rethink the role of religion and government. They came to recognize that the new nation they were creating was indeed a *tabula rasa*—a clean slate upon which they could design a new form of government.

Trinity Church (1726), Newport, Rhode Island.

America was the new Athens, a shining example of democracy to the world. One way to support this ideal was to eliminate the cause of the religious conflicts that had ravaged Europe over the centuries. To do this, Congress in 1789 adopted the First Amendment to the U.S. Constitution, forbidding the introduction of an established church into the New World. As a result, nowhere else in the world can one find the great variety of churches that are seen in North America, and nowhere are there so many different interpretations of what it means to "worship in the beauty of holiness."

CHAPTER ONE
NORTH AMERICAN CHURCH SETTLEMENT

The first Europeans to arrive and establish settlements in the New World were the Spanish. Staunchly Roman Catholic and dedicated to converting the native peoples, Spanish missionaries felt the beauty of holiness resided in the magnificent basilica-type Baroque churches they left behind in their homeland. Therefore, efforts were made to replicate these buildings in the New World, perhaps most successfully in the missions in the West, such as San Xavier del Bac (1769) in Arizona. However, the Spanish Baroque style seen in these buildings did not have a major impact on North American church architecture until the style's nostalgic return in the late 19th and early 20th centuries.

The architects behind early Spanish missions in North America sought to reproduce the stately houses of worship that were the norm in their native country. This philosophy can be seen in 17th- and 18th-century missions in Mexico and present-day border states, including this ornate domed and arched specimen in Arizona. San Xavier del Bac (1769), near Tucson, Arizona.

THE BIRTH OF THE MEETINGHOUSE

The Catholic presence in the New World was soon overshadowed by the arrival of a new group seeking the Promised Land—the Pilgrims who landed on Plymouth Rock in 1620 and the Puritans who followed ten years later to establish the Massachusetts Bay Company and the city of Boston. Rejecting the traditional basilica plan and the traditional church hierarchy and liturgy, the Puritans set out to develop their own unique form of worship and civil space that was not dependent on earlier models. The result was a new architectural creation, the meetinghouse, which became the center of Puritan communal life.

Evidence of the Puritan's success remains visible in Hingham, Massachusetts, in the Old Ship Meetinghouse (started 1681). Currently owned by

TOP RIGHT: **The oldest meetinghouse in continuous ecclesiastical use in the United States, Old Ship's current incarnation is underpinned by a central structure that is more than three centuries old. The austere exterior sheaths an equally plain interior.** Old Ship Meetinghouse (started 1681), Hingham, Massachusetts.

BOTTOM RIGHT: **Old Ship's bare walls and general lack of embellishment put the emphasis squarely on the preacher. Sermons are delivered from the raised pulpit to ensure every member of the congregation can see.** Old Ship Meetinghouse.

CHURCH PLANS

There are basically four major church plans: basilica, broadhouse (meetinghouse), central, and auditorium. It is important to note that a revival of an architectural style does not necessarily mean a revival of its traditional floor plan. New plans are often housed in old skins. Also, while the exterior of a church may promote a congregation's public identity, its plan has to function for its liturgy or religious observance.

Basilica

Primarily favored by such liturgical congregations as Roman Catholics, Lutherans, and Episcopalians, the basilica-plan church is usually rectangular and divided into three basic components—narthex, nave, and chancel—arranged along a longitudinal axis. Typically found in one of the short walls, the entrance opens onto an enclosed narthex that serves as a transition from the secular world to the sacred, or the altar. From there the worshiper enters the nave. The nave may be divided by columns into a broad central section with aisles that provide a pathway toward the raised chancel. The chancel often ends in an apse that projects off the wall opposite the entrance. Additional shrines or altars may line the side chapels and the ambulatory.

Variations of the basilica plan include the cruciform plan (also referred to as the Latin Cross plan), which is created when transepts intersect the nave to create a crossing between the nave and the chancel. Another variation is the hall church where the nave and aisles are of approximately equal height.

Continued on page 10

a Unitarian congregation, the building has been restored to its 1755 appearance. Modest on the exterior, without any Christian symbolism, its equally unadorned interior is broadhouse in plan—its main entrance is in the center of one broad wall; against the opposite wall is the pulpit. Pews on the first floor and galleries along the other three walls face the raised pulpit and allow everyone to see and hear the preacher.

Meetinghouses erected by the Society of Friends, or Quakers, were even more austere than those of the Puritans. Lacking clergy and believing that God spoke to everyone equally, Quaker meetinghouses do not have a pulpit or other symbols of authority. Pictured here is one of the first Quaker meetinghouses in the colonies. Newport Friends Meetinghouse (1699), Newport, Rhode Island.

Continued from page 9

Broadhouse

While meetinghouses may vary in appearance, all are simple in plan and generally modest in size. Often built of wood and painted white, the square or rectangular building may have up to four entrances: one in each wall so people can enter from all directions or separate entrances for men and women. Unlike the basilica plan, the broadhouse plan lacks a longitudinal axis. In rectangular buildings, the pulpit, the building's focus, is placed against one of the broad walls, usually opposite the main entrance. Galleries and pews are arranged so all worshipers have a good view of the pulpit, which is often set on a raised *dais*, or platform. The table for the sacrament is set below the pulpit. Windows are set with clear glass, and all decoration is avoided.

Central

The traditional arrangement for Orthodox Christian churches, the central plan has been gaining favor among Roman Catholics and some Protestant denominations. The plan's primary feature is a dome that crowns the building's central space. In Orthodox churches, the dome symbolizes heaven and is often painted with an image of *Christ Pantocrator* (Christ Triumphant). The space under the dome originally was reserved for clergy and the altar. However, this changed during the 14th century when worshipers began to occupy the space and the altar was moved behind an iconostasis.

Auditorium

Usually square, circular, fan-shape, or octagonal, this type of church plan is entered through a vestibule that opens onto a broad sanctuary with a raked floor. The seats are typically arranged in semicircular arcs facing a pulpit stage that is raised several feet above the main floor. A balcony may wrap around three sides of the hall. Many of these churches have walls that open so those attending Sunday school can hear the preacher.

HEADING SOUTH

The Anglicans' major foothold in the New World was in the southern colonies, where a group of English merchants were granted a royal charter and founded the colony of Virginia in 1606. Virginia is home to nearly 40 colonial-era Anglican churches that remain relatively unchanged, thanks mainly to the fact that many were built of durable brick—unlike the wood religious structures in the North.

A modest replica of the churches English immigrants left behind, Old St. Luke's is the oldest extant Anglican church in the United States. Nicknamed "Old Brick," the church is also the nation's only original Gothic—as opposed to Gothic Revival—religious structure. Old St. Luke's (Historic St. Luke's National Shrine) (ca 1632), near Smithfield, Virginia.

The oldest of these Anglican churches is Old St. Luke's (Historic St. Luke's National Shrine) (started ca 1632) near Smithfield in Isle of Wight County. The medieval Gothic style of this basilica-plan church reveals its builders' efforts to replicate the parish churches and cathedrals they left behind in England on a smaller scale in the New World. In typical Anglican fashion, Old St. Luke's handsome interior includes a chancel rail and rood screen that serve to separate the clergy and altar from the congregation. While its Gothic style reflects the past, this small parish church also anticipates the future. It has several neoclassical features, such as a triangular pediment above the door that reveals its builders' familiarity with the works of England's most distinguished interpreters of the neoclassical style, Sir Christopher Wren and James Gibbs (see page 12).

An arched chancel rail serves as a boundary between clergy and congregation at Old St. Luke's—a detail that was removed from most churches after Vatican II. Old St. Luke's.

WREN, GIBBS, AND THE NEOCLASSICAL STYLE

Sir Christopher Wren (1632–1723) designed St. Paul's Cathedral and many other churches in London following the Great Fire of 1666. Influenced by Italian Renaissance architecture and its use of classical motifs, Wren and his younger colleague, James Gibbs (1682–1754), are responsible for introducing the neoclassical style of architecture to the colonies.

Two main architectural types fall under neoclassical: Georgian and Federal. Georgian, also called English Colonial, dates from 1733, the beginning of the reign of England's King George I, to King George II, who ruled at the time of the American Revolution. Federal refers to the period following the war until about 1840. Both Georgian and Federal architecture borrow features from classical architecture, including pedimented and arched doors and windows, the latter set with clear glass; elaborate cornices and moldings; and sculpted and painted garlands and wreaths. A church designed in the neoclassical style would have typically had a front façade built of wood or brick with a pedimented portico and multistage tower. Neoclassical style's appeal to Americans was its association with the ancient Greek's democratic ideals and republican Rome's constitutional form of government.

In their plan and style, churches designed by Wren and Gibbs combine old and new concepts of the beauty of holiness. This is particularly evident in Gibbs's St. Martin-in-the-Fields (1726) in London, a church that would ultimately have a major impact on the appearance of religious architecture in the New World. When the church's plans and drawings were brought to the New World, they were readily accepted in the colonies' rapidly expanding cities, indicating that material beauty and elegance were now becoming an acceptable part of the worship experience.

Christ Church is called "The Nation's Church" because of the number of the nation's founders who were once in the congregation. The burial ground is the final resting place for many a colonial-era luminary, including Benjamin Franklin. Christ Church (1744), Philadelphia, Pennsylvania.

OPPOSITE: **Designed as an "auditory" church, St. Martin-in-the-Fields lacks the soaring height and length of earlier Gothic churches. Instead, the interior's clear glass windows, galleries, and excellent acoustics allow the preacher to be easily seen and heard. The front façade of the church is familiar to most Americans: a combination of a classically inspired pedimented porch and a Gothic-inspired multi-stage tower surmounted by a steeple.** St. Martin-in-the-Fields (1726), London, England.

Made of wood, clad in clapboard, and painted white or built of red brick with white trim, churches influenced by Wren and Gibbs adorn calendars and travel posters everywhere. Their roots, however, are deep in British soil. Pre-Revolutionary War Anglican examples of Wren/Gibbs-influenced churches include Christ Church (1744) in Philadelphia, Pennsylvania. It features an elaborately decorated exterior with classical details.

In the southern colonies, St. Michael's is considered one of the premier examples of the Georgian style in the United States. Its multistage tower and spire rise 186 feet to its weathervane. St. Michael's Episcopal Church (1761), Charleston, South Carolina.

Following the conclusion of the War for Independence, the Anglican Church was transformed into the Episcopal Church in the United States and Wren/Gibbs' plans were translated into an American idiom by craftspeople like Asher Benjamin, a carpenter who published *The Country Builder's Assistant* in 1797. Now referred to as the Federal style and the American Church Plan, the style and plan moved westward with the frontier where vernacular interpretations were erected.

Close on the heels of Federal style, and often lumped together with it, is Greek Revival, which flourished in the United States from about 1820 to 1840 (although churches continued to be built in this style until the 1860s and beyond). Unlike neoclassical architecture, Greek Revival borrows only from ancient Greek sources. Since Greek temples were built of stone, so too, were many Greek Revival churches. If stone was too expensive, the church was built of wood painted to look like masonry. Even the most modest religious structure boasted at least one Greek feature: for example, a simple gable front, corner pilasters, or a colonnaded portico. Arches were avoided (the Romans invented them); instead, the traditional Greek post-and-lintel method of construction was used.

Americans identified themselves as the keepers of the flame of democracy set ablaze by the ancient Greeks, so they were sympathetic to the Greek's efforts in the 1820s to free themselves from the control of the Ottoman Empire. To show their support, Americans not only named many of their emerging towns after Greek cities (e.g., Athens, Georgia, and Ithaca, New York), but they also began to adorn their buildings with Greek Revival features. Churches were erected with temple fronts but without the neoclassical soaring tower and spire. An outstanding example of this style is St. Peter's Roman Catholic Church (1836) in New York City (see page 45).

THE ROMANTIC MOVEMENT SETTLES IN

The glory days of the Greek Revival style were short. By the mid-19th century, the Industrial Revolution and its byproducts—pollution, poverty, and the growth of overcrowded cities—resulted in what has been called the Romantic Movement, a looking back at the past through rose-colored glasses. Formed by intellectuals at Cambridge and Oxford Universities, the English Ecclesiastical Society sought to revitalize the Anglican church by cleansing it of Reformation "contamination" and to return it to Christianity's "golden era"—the Gothic period, when the church was united and ruled supreme. They argued that the beauty of holiness was not to be found in a church that looked like a "pagan temple" but in the soaring, dimly lit Gothic-style church.

Wary of the influence popular preachers had over the people, Anglicans wanted the church to return to the longitudinal basilica plan with its pointed arches,

Continued on page 19

The steeple for Boston's King's Chapel was never completed, but the chapel's design and decoration is replete with elements favored by Wren and Gibbs, including a high wine-glass pulpit and sounding board. It is also the first church in the colonies to have an organ. King's Chapel (consecrated 1749), Boston, Massachusetts.

COMMON CHURCH TERMS

The following terms are used to describe the many details of the beautiful North American churches featured in this book:

Altar—In Christian churches, a table on supports consecrated for the celebration of the sacrament. Also called a communion table.
Ambulatory—An aisle encircling the apse or choir. An aisle behind the altar.
Apse—A semicircular space that often projects off the eastern end of a church.
Arch—Curved structure spanning an opening. Semicircular round arches used for Romanesque; pointed arches for Gothic.
Ashlar masonry—Hewn blocks of stone.
Attributes—Symbolic objects identifying a saint.
Baldacchino—Canopy over the altar that represents the dome of heaven.
Barrel vault—A continuous arched stone roof or ceiling.
Basilica—Originally a Roman colonnaded hall. Later applied to oblong churches with nave, aisles, and often galleries and an apse on a short wall opposite the main entrance. Also an honorific title conferred by the pope to particular Catholic churches.
Cathedra—Throne for presiding bishop.
Chancel—The east end of a church where liturgy is performed. Traditionally houses the altar.
Clerestory—Clear windows in the upper story of a wall, usually above lower side aisles in basilica-plan buildings.
Colonnade—A row of columns.
Colonnaded portico—A porch with a roof supported on columns. Also known as a pedimented portico.
Corbel—A stone bracket.
Crossing—The center of a church where the nave, transepts, and eastern arm meet.
Crucifix—Cross with crucified Christ figure.
Cruciform—A church plan with one arm longer than the other three. Created when transepts or cross-arms intersect the nave, making a crossing between the nave and chancel. Also known as Latin cross.
Entablature—Horizontal beams resting on columns or pilasters, usually associated with a classical order.
Eucharist—Principal act of worship of the Christian religion; also known as the Divine Liturgy, Holy Communion, Lord's Supper, or Mass.
Façade—Front or principal face of a building.
Flying buttress—A masonry half-arch on the exterior of a building that transmits the thrust of a vault or roof from the upper part of a wall to an outer support or buttress.
Gable—The triangular upper portion of a wall at the end of a pitched roof.
Greek cross—A cross with four arms of equal length.
Icon—Religious images in an Orthodox church. They are objects of veneration and treated with respect.
Iconostasis—In an Orthodox church, a screen displaying icons that separates the priest's area and the altar from the congregation.
Lantern—A structure with windows placed on top of a roof or dome to let in light.
Latin cross—*See Cruciform.*
Liturgical—A form of public worship. In Christian churches, it pertains to denominations whose focus is on the altar where Divine Liturgy (Eucharist) is performed. Includes Roman Catholic, Episcopal, and Lutheran.
Multistage tower—A tower divided into telescoping sections.
Narthex—An enclosed porch that stretches across the entire width of a façade.
Nave—Great central space in a house of worship, often flanked by aisles.
Nonliturgical—Protestant denominations whose focus is on the pulpit instead of the altar. Includes Baptist, Congregational (United Church of Christ), United Methodist, and Presbyterian.

Pediment—The triangular gable at the end of the roof, usually of a portico.
Pedimented portico—*See Colonnaded portico.*
Pilaster—A rectangular column projecting only slightly from a wall.
Portico—A roofed space, open or partly closed, often with columns and a pediment.
Pulpit—Speaking platform from which a pastor delivers the sermon.
Reredos—Screen behind the altar, often decorated with images of saints.
Ribbed vault—A stone ceiling or roof where the groins, or edges, of the vault are outlined by stone.
Rood screen—A beam or screen with a large crucifix, usually located at the entrance to the chancel.
Rose window—Large, circular stained glass window usually on the front façade of Gothic churches.
Sanctuary—Term often used to identify the location of the altar in liturgical churches; the worship space. In Orthodox churches, it refers to the body of the church.
Sounding board—Structure behind or over pulpit.
Stations of the Cross—Fourteen scenes, painted or sculpted in relief or three dimensions, that portray scenes from Jesus' trial and crucifixion. Usually found in Roman Catholic churches.
Tabernacle—In churches, a decorated receptacle that holds the consecrated hosts.
Trabeated—Post-and-lintel (beam) construction used in Greek Revival architecture.
Tracery—Ornamental stonework that holds glass in a window.
Transept—Cross-arms that intersect the nave, creating a crossing between the nave and chancel. The cross-arms usually project beyond the nave.
Vault—Arched ceiling or roof usually of stone or brick.
Vernacular—Buildings erected by local craftspeople.
Vestibule—*See Narthex.*

Continued from page 15

elaborate stained glass windows, and altar set in a deep chancel separated from the nave by a railing. The Anglicans exported their renewed style to the United States, where it found a receptive audience in a nation that was experiencing a Second Great Awakening. The Gothic Revival style was adopted almost immediately by those faiths whose focus is traditionally on the altar: Episcopalians, Roman Catholics, and Lutherans.

Over the years, this style underwent many manifestations; however, certain elements did remain constant, making it relatively easy to identify a Gothic Revival church. While the building techniques of the Middle Ages were not revived, the Gothic style, replete with all of its religious symbolism, was copied. What primarily characterizes a Gothic church is its verticality, created by the use of pointed arches and soaring towers with belfry. A vaulted interior, often with elaborate ribbing, is dimly lit by the sun through large pointed-arch stained glass windows.

The first Gothic Revival church built in the United States under the direct guidance of the English Ecclesiastical Society is the Church of St. James the Less (1846–48) in Philadelphia. (St. Luke's on pages 10–11 was built around 166 years earlier and is not a revival but a continuation of the medieval Gothic style.) Modeled after St. Michael's Longstanton in Cambridgeshire—an early 13th-century English parish church—St. James the Less is small in scale.

A Gothic Revival archetype—and the first medieval parish in the United States—St. James the Less is a faithful reproduction of St. Michael's, Longstanton in Cambridgeshire, England. Church of St. James the Less (1846–48), Philadelphia, Pennsylvania.

OPPOSITE: **The ornate façade of the world's largest Gothic cathedral fronts a church that has been under construction for more than a century. Approximately two-thirds complete as of 2004, St. John the Divine enjoys a local reputation as a church with a love of the arts.** The Cathedral Church of St. John the Divine (started 1892), New York, New York.

Two far more monumental Gothic Revival churches, which were both built in New York City, had a greater impact on popularizing the Gothic Revival style in the United States: Richard Upjohn's Trinity Church (1846) and St. Patrick's Cathedral (1858–76), designed by James Renwick, Jr. (see page 46). Furthering the style's popularity was *Rural Architecture,* a pattern book written by Upjohn in 1852. *Rural Architecture* was carried westward by missionaries and pioneers, and the small churches erected according to the book's plans remain a defining feature in America's heartland.

Gothic Revival churches were constructed in a variety of ethnic styles brought over to the New World by newly arriving immigrants, as well as two so-called modern variations—Victorian and Neo-Gothic. Designed in the rigorously correct Neo-Gothic style are The Cathedral Church of St. John the Divine (started 1892) in New York City and the Cathedral Church of St. Peter and St.

The originator of Richardsonian Romanesque architecture, Henry Hobson Richardson melded ancient styles with modern influences in his masterwork, Trinity Church on Boston's Copley Square. The ornate structure—a bold departure from the 19th-century standard—is now dwarfed by modern structures nearby, including the Hancock Tower and the Boston Public Library. Trinity Church (1877), Boston, Massachusetts.

Paul (started 1907), or Washington National Cathedral, in Washington, D.C. (see pages 62–63).

EVANGELISM AND THE ROMANESQUE REVIVAL

The Second Great Awakening had an enormous impact on nonliturgical congregations whose focus is on the pulpit, not the altar. Passionate, articulate preachers began to attract large numbers of people in the mid-19th century, making it necessary to build more expansive churches to accommodate the crowds. For these Protestant faiths, Greek Revival architecture was "too pagan," but they also believed that Gothic was "too Catholic." Instead they chose the solid and sober Romanesque style that preceded Gothic in the Middle Ages. This style represented an era when Christianity was still under attack by nonbelievers and churches were built to be fortresses with massive stone walls pierced with small, round arched windows and stone barrel-vaulted interiors.

Continued on page 26

The home of the first Methodist congregation organized west of the Mississippi River, Wesley Methodist Church's interior is marked by its auditorium floor plan under a regal dome of stained glass. The impressive façade of the pipe organ behind the pulpit is the 1891 original, while the organ itself is a newer edition. Wesley Methodist Church (1890), Minneapolis, Minnesota.

The Orange County, California, home of Dr. Robert Schuller and his television program, *Hour of Power*, this gleaming glass-and-steel cathedral is clad with 10,000 mirrored windows that swathe an auditorium that seats nearly 3,000. The bell tower (to the right), consisting of polished steel prisms and a 52-bell carillon, was erected in 1990. Garden Grove Community Church (Crystal Cathedral) (1980), Garden Grove, California.

Continued from page 23

Massive towers often flank the main entrances or are placed off to one side.

The Romanesque style's militant character made it attractive to many evangelical faiths who viewed themselves as fighting the forces of darkness that were overtaking their crowded and blighted cities. Building a church was seen as part of a great battle between God's forces, represented by Protestant Christians, and the "unchurched," many of whom were impoverished immigrants. Social reform movements were started, and churches were constructed that were large enough to accommodate a variety of functions, including Sunday schools, kitchens and dining rooms, libraries, and even gymnasiums to keep children off the street.

While the exteriors of the churches during this period were Romanesque Revival, the interiors were not. Rather than the longitudinal basilica-plan that did not work well for preaching, clergy and congregants sought a plan that would accommodate large crowds but would still have excellent acoustics and sight lines. Their solution was the auditorium plan that was gaining popularity in the 19th century for various secular activities. Wesley Methodist Church, built in Minneapolis in 1890, is an excellent example of this style and plan.

Henry Hobson Richardson (1838–86), an American architect who studied at L'école des Beaux-Arts in Paris, developed his own unique variation of the Romanesque Revival style that became known as "Richardsonian Romanesque." He freely borrowed elements from a variety of sources, ancient and contemporary, for the design of his most famous church, Trinity Church (1877) in Boston. John La Farge (1835–1910) designed the entire extravagant interior, including the murals and stained glass windows.

The auditorium-plan church remains very much in vogue, although the Romanesque Revival exterior has been abandoned. "Megachurches," huge complexes that are surrounded by parking lots and can seat thousands, are being built in America's expanding suburbs. One incredible example is the glistening Crystal Cathedral (1980), or Garden Grove Community Church, in Garden Grove, California. Usually nondescript on the exterior and often lacking any Christian symbolism, these auditoriums are designed as theaters with huge stages that can hold orchestras, choruses, and the presiding minister. Additional spaces in the building are set aside for a variety of other functions, from choir rooms to snack shops and even bowling alleys.

Nineteenth-century romanticism saw the revival of other styles, including Byzantine, a style that is usually associated with Orthodox Christianity but is also used by other Christian denominations. However, there is a difference. For Orthodox Christians this style did not need a "revival"—their churches have been built almost continuously in variations of this style for well over a thousand years. Orthodox Greek churches are usually in the shape of a Greek Cross (a cross with four equal arms) and crowned with a dome. On the other hand, Orthodox churches in Eastern Europe are generally divided into three sections in a linear fashion—entry, nave, and sanctuary—and are topped by small onion domes and three-barred orthodox crosses. In all Orthodox churches the sanctuary is closed off by an iconostasis.

THE NEW CLASSICAL: BEAUX-ARTS STYLE

One last 19th-century style must be discussed, and it was less a revival than a philosophy taught at L'école des Beaux-Arts in Paris. The principles of the academy were based on the belief that "new" architecture should be an extension of the classical tradition, particularly that of Roman antiquity and the Italian Renaissance. Imposing in size, churches of the Beaux-Arts period were typically built of stone or brick. They display an array of architectural features, including grand staircases often flanked with sculptural figures leading up to elaborately decorated façades; ornamented towers at times capped with spires or onion domes; or a large central dome placed above the crossing. The interiors are equally elaborate, featuring rich materials like marble and mosaic. The walls may be covered with paintings or sculpture, and light enters through stained glass windows. The Beaux-Arts style became popular in the United States after many of the buildings in the "Great White City" at the 1893 World's Columbian Exposition in Chicago were built using these principles.

Emmanuel Masqueray (1861–1917), a French architect who trained at L'école and was chief of design for the Louisiana Purchase Exposition in St. Louis in 1904, designed a number of Catholic churches in the Midwest in the Beaux-Arts style. The Basilica of St. Mary (1907–15) in Minneapolis is a stellar example.

MODERN MOVEMENT

The 20th century witnessed the birth of modernism and a search for a new architectural vocabulary. Many major architects began to design churches that were not dependent upon earlier styles. Frank Lloyd Wright's search resulted in the magnificent Unity Temple (1906–09) in Oak Park, Illinois, for his own Unitarian congregation (see pages 29 and 82). He extended his vocabulary even further when he reinvented the appearance of a Greek Orthodox Church in his design for Annunciation Greek Orthodox Church (1956) outside Milwaukee, Wisconsin.

Eliel Saarinen, the great Finnish architect, completely revised the appearance of Protestant church architecture with his simple but elegant design of First Christian Church (1942) in Columbus, Indiana. Its impressive bell tower, a community landmark, competes for attention

OPPOSITE: **The oldest basilica in the United States, the Basilica of St. Mary takes up nearly an entire city block in downtown Minneapolis and is regarded as an archetype of the Beaux-Arts architectural style. The dome started leaking in the 1980s, leading to a comprehensive restoration.** Basilica of St. Mary (1907–15), Minneapolis, Minnesota.

with the dramatic spire his son Eero used in his design for the equally impressive North Christian Church in Columbus. First Christian's interior features a traditional basilica plan with altar and pulpit at the far end of the nave (see page 83).

Increasing inventiveness in church design characterized the years following World War II as Americans rushed to the suburbs. Suburban churches were designed to serve a variety of functions, beyond worship services. Sprawling complexes were constructed, many in designs that refused to look "religious" in character. Enormous roofs became fashionable, displacing the walls and eliminating windows.

Continued on page 33

Frank Lloyd Wright referred to this geometrically striking church as his "jewel box." He designed Unity Temple for his own Unitarian congregation after its modest wooden predecessor burned in 1905. Unity Temple (1906–09), Oak Park, Illinois.

Renowned architect Frank Lloyd Wright combined traditional elements with a radical circular design to create a Greek Orthodox church for the 20th century. The primary motif is the Greek cross emblazoned with a circle: It is the basis of the floor plan and also seen in many decorative features. Annunciation Greek Orthodox Church (1956), Wauwatosa, Wisconsin.

GREEK ORTHODOX CHURCH

Built from a design by Finnish architect Eliel Saarinen and his son Eero, First Christian Church was the first contemporary structure in Columbus, Indiana, and was also one of the first modern churches in the United States. The stark, geometric exterior is primarily limestone and buff brick. First Christian Church (1942), Columbus, Indiana.

The shell-like form of the United Church of Rowayton takes cues from a common image in the surrounding area. A district in Norwalk, Connecticut, Rowayton is a coastal community at the mouth of the Five Mile River. United Church of Rowayton (1962), Rowayton, Connecticut.

Continued from page 29

Refusing to look to the past, some architects chose instead to look at their own environment for inspiration. For example, the shell-like form of the United Church of Rowayton (1962) in Connecticut refers to its location in a small coastal village.

The inventiveness that characterized the years following World War II unexpectedly resulted in a backlash when many in the next generation complained that their churches didn't look "churchlike"; they lacked the elusive quality referred to as the beauty of holiness. The question this raises is what is "churchlike"? As we have seen, many North American churches do not fall into neat categories. They display the sense of freedom that characterizes the American spirit. The search for a more "churchlike" building coincides with the onset of the postmodern era

In response to contemporary churches that did not look "churchlike" enough, the congregation of the Church of St. Therese got what they asked for. The conventional brick basilica with a steep roof and narrow windows conform to the standards espoused by Vatican II. Church of St. Therese (1989), Wilson, North Carolina.

that began in the 1970s when the inventiveness of the post-war era merged with a desire to return to more traditional designs.

In response to a Roman Catholic congregation's request for a church that looks like a church, the architects of the Church of St. Therese (1989) in Wilson, North Carolina, designed a traditional brick cruciform basilica with a steep roof and narrow windows. The altar, located in the crossing underneath a traditional lantern and spire, conforms to the dictates of Vatican II.

The return to the past for inspiration does not mean that architects have ceased to be inventive. The Marilyn Moyer Meditation Chapel (1991) in Portland, Oregon, is perched atop a nearly vertical 130-foot-high cliff offering a spectacular setting for meditation.

The reconciliation of opposites is what church architects have always been asked to do. The sacred spaces these artists design are intended to embrace worshipers in the beauty of holiness in all of its many interpretations.

OPPOSITE: **Atop a sheer cliff, the Marilyn Moyer Meditation Chapel is a relatively new addition to The National Sanctuary of Our Sorrowful Mother, commonly known as The Grotto. The chapel's north wall consists exclusively of glass, allowing for a breathtaking view of the Cascade Mountains.** Marilyn Moyer Meditation Chapel (1991), Portland, Oregon.

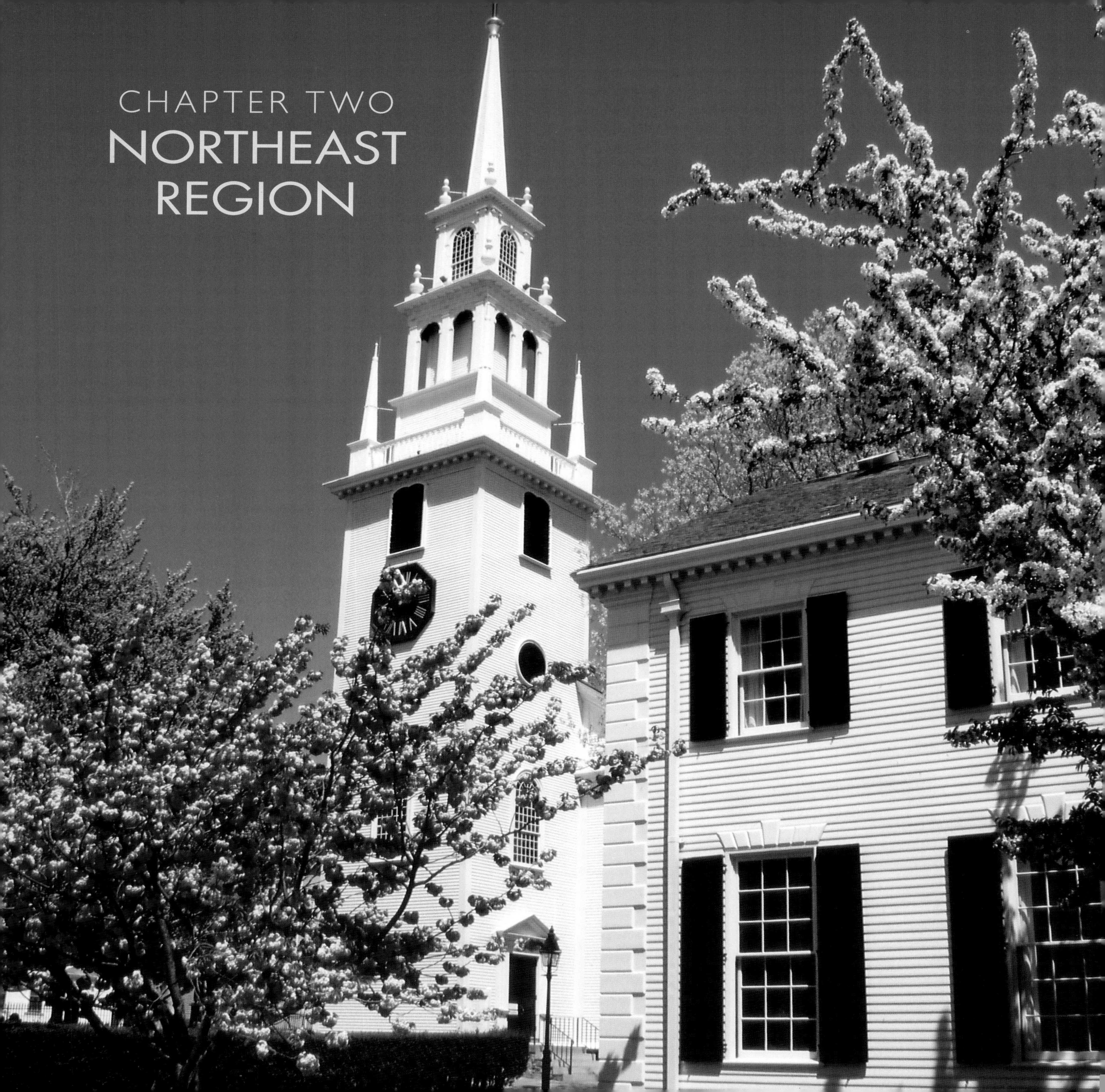

CHAPTER TWO

NORTHEAST REGION

The image most people have when they think of churches in the northeastern region of the United States is the colonial "church on the village green," such as the much-photographed First Church of Christ (Center Church) on the Common (1812–14) in New Haven, Connecticut (see page 42). But from the time the first Europeans set foot on its shores and grasped the potential this vast wilderness had to offer, the Northeast has attracted people representing a vast diversity of beliefs and ethnicities.

OPPOSITE: **Perched above Newport Harbor, Trinity is the oldest Anglican church in Rhode Island. The pictured white clapboard structure replaced the parish's original church (1700) in 1726, was expanded in 1762, and was painstakingly renovated in the 1980s.** Trinity Church (1726), Newport, Rhode Island.

NEW WORLD, NEW RELIGIOUS FREEDOM

The first settlers in New England were the Pilgrims and Puritans, who argued for reform of the Church of England and were determined to establish a holy commonwealth for like-minded people in the New World. They wanted Christianity to return to the simplicity of the early church, where there was no distinction between civil and religious institutions. Arguing against the elaborate ritual and churches of the Anglicans, the Puritans chose to call their religious buildings meetinghouses—a term that better reflected their multipurpose nature. Old Ship Meetinghouse (1681) in Hingham, Massachusetts, is the only Puritan meetinghouse still standing (see page 8).

The Religious Society of Friends, also called the Quakers, developed out of the Puritan reform movement in England. The term Quaker comes from a comment

This Quaker meetinghouse is basic inside and out so parishioners can focus on their "inner light." An 1895 Elwood Roberts poem described the church with the stanza, "In shade of buttonwoods and oaks/The plain, old-fashioned building stands." Horsham Friends Meetinghouse (1803), Montgomery County, Pennsylvania.

NEAR RIGHT: **Built by early Dutch settlers as a house of worship for the working class, this modest fieldstone structure is the oldest extant church in New York State. It is located near the onetime home of Washington Irving and adjacent to the Sleepy Hollow Cemetery.** The Old Dutch Reformed Church of Sleepy Hollow (1702), North Tarrytown, New York.

FAR RIGHT: **A more elaborate structure built by the Dutch Reformed Church is the First Reformed Church of Hackensack—the congregation's third church built on the same site. Remodeled over the years, the church is built of local sandstone and displays characteristics of the Wren/Gibbs-inspired Federal style combined with Gothic Revival pointed windows.** First Reformed Church of Hackensack (1791), Hackensack, New Jersey.

made by its founder, George Fox, who said that one should tremble at the word of God. Quakers believe that God approaches everyone directly through the "inner light" that is the Christ within. Like the Puritans, they preferred simple, unadorned spaces for worship.

One example is Horsham Friends Meetinghouse (1803) in Montgomery County, Pennsylvania. Its simple exterior matches the inside of the structure, which features a balcony encircling the entire interior. The Quaker meetinghouse retains virtually all of its original details.

SHAKERS

An offshoot of the Quakers is the United Society of Believers in Christ's Second Coming, known simply as the Shakers. The society's nickname came about because of its members' habit of shaking, dancing, singing, and shouting during worship. One of the great Shaker prophets was Mother Ann Lee, who fled England in 1774 and settled in Watervliet, New York. By 1794 there were 12 Shaker villages in New England. Today, because of the faith's vows of celibacy and lack of new members, only one meetinghouse survives—the Sabbathday Lake Meetinghouse (1794) in Sabbathday, Maine. Although pews were added to the interior in 1900, the center of the hall remains open for the Shaker worship practice of dancing and marching.

The Dutch settled along the coast of New England in 1624 and established the Dutch Reformed Church and a harbor named New Amsterdam. A wealthy family of landowners erected The Old Dutch Reformed Church of Sleepy Hollow (1702) in North Tarrytown, New York. The rubble-stone church is very simple in design; its only ornamentations are a small bell tower on the roof and pointed Gothic Revival windows, which were a later addition to the building.

German pietists established the New World's first Protestant monastery in 1735, the Ephrata Cloister in Ephrata, Pennsylvania. Built in the steeped-roof style of the medieval architecture of its founders' homeland, the cloister's three main buildings are the *Saal,* or chapel, the *Saron,* or Sisters' House, and the *Bethania,* or Brothers' House.

ANGLICANS AND THE WREN/GIBBS STYLE

The British-supported Society for the Propagation of the Gospel in Foreign Parts began to make inroads in the Northeast region in the 1700s, thanks in part to the fact that many prominent colonists were Anglican, including George Washington, James Madison, Patrick Henry, and 34 signers of the Declaration of Independence. Anglican churches began to proliferate, and many of these religious structures reveal their builders' awareness of the Wren/Gibbs style.

Founded by 18th-century German immigrants, the Ephrata Cloister was the first Protestant monastery in what is now the United States. The cloister was originally a communal society with three orders: monks, nuns, and a married order of "householders." Ephrata Cloister (1735), Ephrata, Pennsylvania.

The red brick Christ Church (Old North) (1723) in Boston, Massachusetts, is perhaps best known for the role it played in America's War for Independence. From its soaring tower were hung the lanterns that warned of the British attack: "One if by land, two if by sea. . . ." The white clapboard structure Trinity Church (1726) in Newport, Rhode Island, is similar to Old North, including its basilica plan and tower (see page 36). Inside, Trinity's large three-stage freestanding pulpit all but obscures the altar that stands behind a chancel rail.

Christ Church (1727–44) in Philadelphia is famous for its elaborate Georgian style and its founders, many of whom contributed to the formation of the new nation (see page 13). The church's beautiful wineglass pulpit was built by a Philadelphia cabinetmaker. Other Wren/Gibbs-inspired religious structures include two designed by Peter Harrison, who is considered the United State's first "professional architect": King's Chapel (1749–54) in Boston and Christ Church (1759–61) in Cambridge, Massachusetts. Founded in 1688 as an Anglican congregation and named in honor of King George I, King's Chapel

OPPOSITE: **In Richmond, Vermont, the community felt it was too small for each denomination to have its own church, so they decided to put their prejudices aside and build only one. Old Round Church, built by five denominations—Baptist, Christian, Congregational, Methodist, and Universalist—remained in use until 1880.** Old Round Church (1813), Richmond, Vermont.

"One if by land, two if by sea." The steeple of this landmark Boston redbrick is irrevocably linked with Paul Revere: It was here on April 18, 1775, that sexton Robert Newman hung two lanterns to warn of the route of British soldiers in the days leading up to the Revolutionary War. Christ Church (Old North) (1723), Boston, Massachusetts.

FAR RIGHT: **Located on Harvard Square, Christ Church has been visited by George Washington, Teddy Roosevelt, and Martin Luther King, Jr., over the course of its existence. Architect Peter Harrison designed the structure to be literally cut in half and expanded, which occurred when the congregation outgrew it in the mid-19th century.** Christ Church (1759–61), Cambridge, Massachusetts.

became the first Unitarian church in America in 1787 (see pages 16–17).

Following the Revolutionary War, Congregationalists began to adopt the neoclassical style, now known as Federal. Examples abound throughout New England, including the white clapboard First Congregational Church (1829) in Litchfield, Connecticut (see page 44).

GREEK REVIVAL MOVES IN

Around 1820, as the popularity of the Federal style waned, the Greek Revival style came into vogue. A

A prototype colonial New England "church on the village green," the First Church of Christ is actually the fourth meetinghouse built on the site. The first services were held outdoors here in 1638, and there is a cemetery on site with gravestones dating back to 1687. First Church of Christ (1812–14), New Haven, Connecticut.

METHODISM AND AFRICAN AMERICANS

John Wesley, an Anglican priest who wanted to make the Church of England more responsive to the needs of the poorer classes, founded Methodism in 1738. In 1784, the first Methodist Episcopal Church in the New World was organized by Francis Asbury in Baltimore, Maryland. Soon Methodist circuit-riding ministers were carrying the gospel on horseback throughout the new nation. Among their converts were many ex-slaves who were often not welcomed into all-white Methodist congregations. As a result, they began to form their own churches. Ex-slaves under the leadership of an African American preacher named Thomas Paul built the African Meeting House (1806) in Boston. The handsome building was remodeled in 1855 and for a time was used as a synagogue. It, along with the African Meeting House (1825) in Nantucket, Massachusetts, was acquired in the 1970s and restored as Museums of Afro American History. Another ex-slave, Richard Allen, founded Mother Bethel African Methodist Episcopal Church (A.M.E.) in Philadelphia in 1787. The congregation's first worship space was an abandoned blacksmith shop. Allen used its anvil as a pulpit; it became the symbol of the A.M.E. Church. The congregation dedicated its current Romanesque Revival–style church in 1890.

FAR LEFT: **The widespread popularity of the neoclassical Wren/Gibbs-style had an impact on churches being built or remodeled by other faiths, including First Baptist Church. Although the structure exhibits a basilica plan and has a temple front and soaring tower, it retains elements from earlier meetinghouses, including entrances in the center of its two broad walls.** First Baptist Church (1775), Providence, Rhode Island.

LEFT: **Surrounded today by skyscrapers, St. Paul's Chapel of Trinity Episcopal Church is another outstanding church in the Federal style. Dedicated in 1766, it is New York City's oldest public building in continuous use. It is beautifully maintained and still has its original elaborate altar and pulpit and all but one of the original Waterford crystal chandeliers.** St. Paul's Chapel (dedicated 1766), New York, New York.

church that illustrates the widespread appeal of this style is St. Peter's Roman Catholic Church (1837) in New York City (see page 45). Its façade could easily be mistaken for a Greek temple, except for the statue of St. Peter set into its pediment and the large cross at its peak. Initially the church had clear glass windows that were later replaced with stained glass.

A far more modest example is the William Miller Chapel, erected in 1848 near Fairhaven, New York, by followers of William Miller, who predicted the coming

Originating in 17th-century London, the Wren/Gibbs neoclassical style migrated into the New World after the Revolutionary War, first in Anglican churches and later in those of other denominations. First Congregational is a prime example of the Wren/Gibbs tradition, marked by its pillared façade, lofty bell tower, and basilica-base floor plan. First Congregational Church (1829), Litchfield, Connecticut.

of Christ before the millennium. The small white clapboard structure features several Greek Revival characteristics on its exterior, including a gable front and corner pilasters.

The birthplace of Adventism, the William Miller Chapel, located on the upstate New York farm of the same name, was named for a Baptist preacher who predicted the coming of Jesus in 1844. His followers built the chapel four years later, when the movement continued to predict the return of Christ. William Miller Chapel (1848), Fairhaven, New York.

ANOTHER ARRIVAL FROM ENGLAND: GOTHIC REVIVAL

The revival of the Gothic style reached the New World in the first decades of the 19th century. Two excellent examples of this style include St. Patrick's Cathedral and Trinity Church. Both are located in New York City, and both were constructed in the 1800s—Trinity Church was dedicated in 1846; construction on St. Patrick's Cathedral started in 1858. English architect Richard Upjohn designed Trinity Church, while St. Patrick's Cathedral was designed by American architect James Renwick, Jr.

Six imposing ionic columns front the Greek Revival home of the oldest Catholic parish in New York City—St. Peter's Roman Catholic Church (1837). The structure is located in Lower Manhattan, just a block away from the site of the World Trade Center. St. Peter's Roman Catholic Church (1837), New York, New York.

Many of the immigrants coming to the United States in the mid-19th century were familiar with the medieval Gothic style in their homelands. When they had the means, these groups would erect a religious structure that was reminiscent of the one they left behind. These buildings are not so much a revival of a style as they are a reinterpretation of it in a new environment using whatever material and technology were available and affordable at the time.

FAR RIGHT: **The majestic spire capping this Gothic Revival archetype—consecrated on Ascension Day in 1846—once dominated the skyline of what is now Manhattan's financial district. The sumptuous interior is marked by an elevated altar, elaborate reredos, and ornate stained glass windows.** Trinity Church (dedicated 1846), New York, New York.

THE ROMANESQUE REVIVAL

Most nonliturgical churches had large auditoriums and were built in the Romanesque Revival or Richardsonian Romanesque style. A good example of this is the Church of Christ, Scientist (1879). Roman Catholics were also familiar with the Romanesque style in their native lands, but for them the style's appeal was more than fashion or nostalgia. A Romanesque-style structure's fortresslike appearance provided its worshipers, many of whom were Eastern European or Irish immigrants, with a sense of security in what they perceived as a hostile society.

RIGHT: **Designed by American architect James Renwick, Jr., this Gothic Revival masterwork features magnificent stained glass, including a great rose window designed by Charles Connick.** St. Patrick's Cathedral (1858–76), New York, New York.

THE BEAUTY OF BYZANTINE

Nineteenth-century Romanticism may have contributed to the choice of the Byzantine style for the extension added to the Church of Christ, Scientist in Boston, or it may have been due to an awareness of churches being erected by Orthodox Christians. Magnificent examples include St. Nicholas Russian Orthodox Cathedral (1902) in New York City, whose elaborate style is described as "Moscow Baroque." Holy Cross Orthodox Church (1988) in Williamsport, Pennsylvania, revives the plan and the timber-and-shingle construction found in Orthodox churches erected in rural areas of Eastern Europe. Not all Orthodox churches are in the Byzantine style, however. The Greek Orthodox Christians in New York City who erected the Greek Orthodox Archdiocesan Cathedral of the Holy Trinity (1933) elected to build a church with the traditional Greek Cross plan crowned with a dome but to enclose it within a Romanesque Revival exterior.

The Christian Scientist church in Boston is not the only non-Orthodox church built in this style. Other congregations tired of the Gothic and Romanesque Revival styles found Byzantine architecture's link to early Christianity appealing. For example, the Episcopal parishioners of St. Bartholomew's in New York City selected the Greek Cross plan and elaborate decoration of the 11th-century San Marco's in Venice, Italy, for their new church designed by Bertram Goodhue.

Mary Baker Eddy founded the Church of Christ, Scientist in 1879. A Romanesque Revival church was erected in 1894 that is now part of The Christian Science Center. A large Byzantine-style extension was added in 1906. The entire complex is centered on a large plaza and reflecting pool, which was completed in the 1960s. Church of Christ, Scientist (1879), Boston, Massachusetts.

LITURGICAL AND NONLITURGICAL DENOMINATIONS

While it could be argued that all churches are liturgical to some degree, Christian denominations are traditionally divided into two groups: liturgical, or ritual, and nonliturgical, or nonritual. Liturgical denominations include Roman Catholic, Episcopal (Anglican), and Lutheran. The focus of their liturgy is on the altar—the site of the sacrament—which is usually located in a chancel. Nonliturgical (or nonritual) refers to Protestant denominations, including Baptist, Methodist, Presbyterian, or Congregational (United Church of Christ). These groups place the emphasis of their liturgy on listening to the Word, or the preacher's sermon. The interior arrangement of a church will reflect a denomination's liturgical practice.

FAR RIGHT: **Capped by onion-shape domes, St. Nicholas Cathedral's opulent Byzantine façade envelops the heart of Russian Orthodoxy in the United States. The first donation that went toward the construction budget came from Czar Nicholas II.** St. Nicholas Russian Orthodox Cathedral (1902), New York, New York.

POST-WORLD WAR II MODERNISM

Churches built following World War II reveal the inventiveness of architects searching for a new architectural vocabulary. Eero Saarinen designed the austere circular Kresge Chapel (1953–55) for the Massachusetts Institute of Technology at Cambridge. Surrounded by a moat and capped by a spire designed by Theodore Roszak, the chapel's windowless interior is illuminated by light filtering through an oculus window in the center of the ceiling.

The Christian symbol of the fish accounts for the shape of First Presbyterian Church (1958) in Stamford, Connecticut. The fish shape is apparent both in the profile and in the floor plan of the church.

RIGHT: **Architect Bertram Goodhue borrowed from both Romanesque and Byzantine influences in designing this Manhattan landmark. In 1981, the city fought St. Bartholomew's plan to develop an adjacent parcel into a skyscraper; the U.S. Supreme Court ultimately upheld the parcel's landmark status and blocked construction.** St. Bartholomew's (1923), New York, New York.

OPPOSITE: **A modern example of Byzantine-influenced architecture, Holy Cross Orthodox Church is based on the same timber-and-shingle tenet that guided similar—albeit considerably older—churches in Eastern Europe.** Holy Cross Orthodox Church (1988), Williamsport, Pennsylvania.

THE POSTMODERN ERA

Architects and clients seeking to reestablish a link with the past began once again to incorporate historic features into their church designs—but this time using modern material and technology. One example, Living Rock Church (1990), located in the rural town of Killingworth, Connecticut, borrows its basilica plan from the Gothic Revival and its simple white clapboard exterior and clear glass windows from the region's Puritan ancestors. Its design brings church architecture in the Northeast region back full circle.

TOP RIGHT: **The conspicuously modern design of First Presbyterian Church incorporates the image of the fish—a symbol that dates from early Christianity (this photo shows the tail and just part of the fish "body"). The stained glass panels that dominate the side depict the Crucifixion and the Resurrection.** First Presbyterian Church (1958), Stamford, Connecticut.

BOTTOM RIGHT: **Another amazing feature of First Presbyterian Church is the fish-shape structure's brilliant sanctuary. Its windows contain more than 20,000 pieces of stained glass.** First Presbyterian Church.

NEAR RIGHT: **Eero Saarinen designed this contemporary round redbrick chapel on the Massachusetts Institute of Technology campus, skirted by varied arches and topped by a knife-like aluminum spire and a circular skylight. The structure was built in tandem with Kresge Auditorium, another striking M.I.T. landmark by Saarinen.** Kresge Chapel (1953–55), Cambridge, Massachusetts.

The colors of fall stand in direct contrast to the stark white exterior of Living Rock Church. The modern structure combines elements of Gothic Revival with the simpler styles favored by Connecticut's early Puritan settlers. Living Rock Church (1990), Killingworth, Connecticut.

CHAPTER THREE

SOUTH ATLANTIC REGION

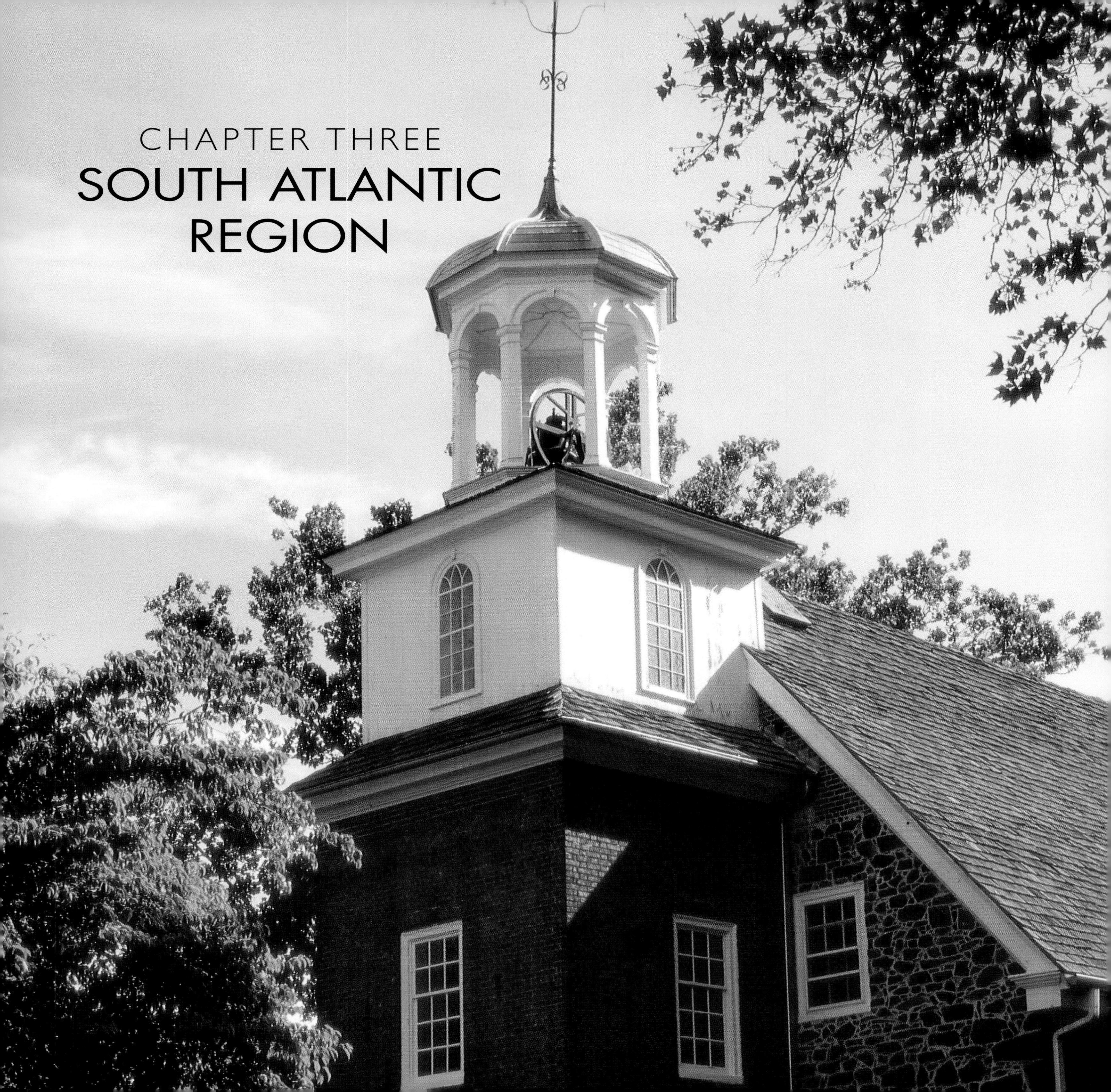

This vast region encompasses several subcultures that are traditionally identified collectively as "the South." Delaware, the region's northernmost state, was settled by Reformed Dutch, Lutheran Swedes, Welsh Baptists, and English Quakers. At the region's southernmost tip is Florida, which was claimed for Spain by Juan Ponce de Leon. British subjects loyal to the Church of England settled a great portion of the central part of the region, including Virginia and North Carolina. The indentured servants who arrived with them were mainly Scotch-Irish and Welsh and were of the Presbyterian and Methodist faiths. Maryland was founded as a refuge for Roman Catholics, who were unwelcome in the other colonies, but over half of its first settlers were Protestant. Georgia, the last colony established by the English, became home to debtors and religious refugees fleeing persecution in Europe.

OPPOSITE: **Constructed of granite with a "jerkinhead" roof (a gable roof with clipped ends), Old Swedes' simple rectangular building features several additions to its original structure, including porches, a gallery, stained glass windows, and a belfry.** Holy Trinity Church (Old Swedes) (1698–99), Wilmington, Delaware.

THE EARLY SETTLERS

The Swedish colony Fort Christina was established in 1638 on the site of what is now Wilmington, Delaware, and Holy Trinity Church (1698–99), also called "Old Swedes," was the colony's centerpiece. Following the Revolutionary War, the Swedish government withdrew its support for Lutheran churches in the United States, and control of Old Swedes was transferred to the new Episcopal Church in America. The church's original black walnut wineglass pulpit

RIGHT: **Dubbed "the cradle of American Methodism," Barratt's Chapel was the first church built by and for Methodists in the United States. The brick structure appears very much as it did in the 1780s. Today, there is a museum within detailing the history of New World Methodism.** Barratt's Chapel (1780), near Frederica, Delaware.

and sounding board remain intact, and its silver communion cup, paten, and wafer box, sent from Sweden in 1718, are still in use.

Meanwhile, circuit-riding Methodist preachers were expanding their reach throughout the South Atlantic region, ministering to the needs of settlers living in isolated areas. However, if Methodists wished to receive the sacraments, they had to attend an Anglican church. This rule changed on November 14, 1784, when an ordained Methodist minister, Thomas Coke, administered the sacraments for the first time in the United States at Barratt's Chapel (1780), near Frederica, Delaware.

Now a Methodist Shrine, Barratt's Chapel is known as the "cradle of American Methodism" because of an event that occurred there one month later: Reverend Coke and the Reverend Francis Asbury called a conference for all

After relocating to North Carolina from Pennsylvania, Moravian settlers erected this stucco-and-stone church, also known as "Gemein Haus," or meetinghouse. The church was in regular use from 1788 to 1953; today, it is only open to the public for special events. Bethabara Moravian Church (Gemein Haus) (1788), Winston-Salem, North Carolina.

Alexander Campbell broke off from the Presbyterian then the Baptist church before founding the Disciples of Christ and building this West Virginia house of worship in 1832. The simple, unadorned church retains its original raised pulpit and separate box pews for men and women. Old Bethany Church (Bethany Church of Christ) (1852), Bethany, West Virginia.

Methodist clergy to meet at the chapel; the result of that meeting was the formation of the Methodist Episcopal Church in America. A metal star placed in the floor at the opening of the chancel rail marks the spot of their meeting.

North Carolina's rugged coastline and mountainous terrain made it attractive to only the most hardy or desperate colonists, including groups trying to escape the notice of British authorities. One such group was the German-speaking Moravians, who settled in North Carolina in the mid-18th century and erected Bethabara Moravian Church (1788) in Winston-Salem. The stuccoed stone building is designed to serve two functions that are differentiated by a shift in the roof line: a meetinghouse, or *saal,* and the pastor's residence. Set on the

FAR LEFT: **Topped by a square wooden belfry, the one-story brick Jerusalem Lutheran Church is simple in design, but its builders' abilities are evident in the structure's skilled crafting. Today it is Georgia's oldest surviving religious structure.** Jerusalem Lutheran Church (1767), New Ebenezer, Georgia.

ridgeline of the meetinghouse is a small arcaded octagonal tower.

Among the settlers welcomed by James Edward Oglethorpe, the founder of the colony of Georgia, were 78 Protestants fleeing persecution in Roman Catholic Salzburg, Austria. They founded the town of New Ebenezer in 1734 and later built Jerusalem Lutheran Church (1767) themselves, including making bricks from river clay.

Scotch-Irish, Welsh, and Germans settled West Virginia in the 1730s. Fiercely independent, many were freed indentured servants who heartily disliked their Anglican overlords. Alexander Campbell, an Irish immigrant who became dissatisfied with what he viewed as the liberalism of the Presbyterian Church in the colonies, decided to become a Baptist preacher and form his own conservative congregation. The Baptist association did not agree with his interpretation of doctrine and withdrew support from his church. In response, Campbell formed a separate denomination, the Disciples of Christ, and built a meetinghouse, Old Bethany Church (Bethany Church of Christ) in Bethany, West Virginia, in 1832. Twenty years later, a prim brick replacement went up on the same foundation. It is still used to this day on special occasions.

Few American churches have as rich of a history as St. Peter's, where George and Martha Washington were married in 1759. A century later, General Robert E. Lee was in the congregation, both before and after the Civil War. He led a drive for the church's renovation after its desecration during the war. St. Peter's Episcopal Church (1701), New Kent County, Virginia.

ANGLICANS AND THE WREN/GIBBS STYLE

The oldest and wealthiest of all the colonies in the South Atlantic region, Virginia was established by colonists loyal to the Church of England and, by 1632, had 15,000 settlers. Unlike much of the Northeast region that was rapidly urbanized, the Anglicans, their indentured servants, and slaves forcibly brought from Africa settled on vast plantations. Small wooden churches were hastily constructed to serve their needs. As soon as money was available, the wooden structures were often replaced by more durable brick and stone buildings.

One example of these churches is St. Peter's Episcopal Church (1701) in New Kent County, Virginia. A belfry was added between 1722 and 1740—an indication of its members' awareness of the new Wren/Gibbs neoclassical style. This small brick church was the site of the marriage of George Washington to the widow Martha Dandridge Custis on January 6, 1759.

Jamestown, the colony's capital, was damaged by fire in 1698, forcing the capital to be moved to Williamsburg, where Bruton Parish Church (1710–15) was built. Its large size attests to its sizable congregation and its need

Originally erected without a tower, one was added to Bruton Parish Church in 1769 to house the "Liberty Bell of Virginia," which was rung to announce the signing of the Declaration of Independence in Philadelphia. Bruton Parish Church (1710–15), Williamsburg, Virginia.

to accommodate royal functions required as the "chapel royal" of Virginia. Unlike the broad rectangular plan favored by Gibbs and used for St. Martin-in-the-Fields, this church is a cruciform (Latin cross) basilica, one of the first in the colonies to have transepts projecting off its broad walls between the nave and chancel.

Georgian decorative details favored by Wren and Gibbs are found throughout St. James Episcopal Church (1719) in Goose Greek, South Carolina. Built by wealthy plantation owners from the West Indies, the stuccoed brick structure features a jerkinhead roof and is decorated with small cherub heads on the keystones above its arched windows. Over its pedimented entrance is a carving of a mother pelican feeding her young, an emblem of the Society for the Propagation of the Gospel in Foreign Parts. The elaborate interior includes a large wineglass pulpit and sounding board situated in front of a reredos that consists of pairs of pilasters supporting a broken pediment bearing the royal arms of King George I.

FAR RIGHT: **The chancel of St. Michael's Episcopal Church was badly damaged at the start of the Civil War but was quickly rebuilt. In 1905, a beautiful stained glass window created in the Tiffany studios was placed in the Palladian window behind the altar.** St. Michael's Episcopal Church (1752–61), Charleston, South Carolina.

Now considered one of the best-preserved English churches in the United States, St. James was restored in the 1840s after decades of abandonment. Services are held once a year in the church, which features a wineglass pulpit and a timeworn coat of royal arms. St. James Episcopal Church (1719), Goose Greek, South Carolina.

In Charleston, South Carolina, the famed St. Michael's Episcopal Church (1761) is considered a premier example of the Wren/Gibbs style (see above and page 14). For a time its triple-tiered tower topped with a triangular sphere served as a lighthouse to help guide ships into the harbor. Its interior is equally impressive: A beautifully carved raised pulpit and sounding board stands to the side of the semicircular apse that houses the chancel.

Neoclassical in design but not to be mistaken for the Wren/Gibbs style of churches preferred by Protestants, Baltimore Cathedral is a huge Latin cross basilica. A large shallow dome, modeled after the dome of the Pantheon in Rome, hovers over the crossing. Basilica of the Assumption of the Blessed Virgin Mary (Baltimore Cathedral) (1804–18), Baltimore, Maryland.

In 1632, King Charles I of England gave George Calvert, the Baron of Baltimore, deed to what would become the colony of Maryland. Lord Baltimore was a Roman Catholic and saw the need for a separate colony where Catholics could worship free of persecution. His dream was short-lived; the Act of Establishment of 1692 that made the Church of England the state-supported religion resulted in Catholicism being outlawed.

Forbidden to build a church, the Catholic minority managed to survive in Maryland and became a vital center for Catholicism in the colonies. In 1789, Baltimore became the seat of the national Catholic diocese, and John Carroll became its first bishop. By 1804 Carroll felt confident enough to hire Benjamin Henry Latrobe, one of the nation's premier architects, to design the Basilica of the Assumption of the Blessed Virgin Mary (Baltimore Cathedral) (1804–18).

The architect of the Baltimore Cathdral, Benjamin Latrobe, presented two designs for the church—a neoclassical version, which was chosen and is shown here, and a Gothic design. Basilica of the Assumption of the Blessed Virgin Mary.

South Carolina native Robert Mills, the architect behind the Washington Monument, designed this Greek Revival gem, nicknamed the "House of Five Porches." The granite monument out front memorializes Revolutionary War hero Jean DeKalb. Bethesda Presbyterian Church (1822), Camden, South Carolina.

THE GREEK REVIVAL, SOUTHERN STYLE

The Greek Revival style arrived early in the South, thanks in part to the efforts of Robert Mills, a student of Latrobe and Thomas Jefferson. Well known for his design of the Washington Monument and other neoclassical buildings in Washington, D.C., Mills agreed to design Bethesda Presbyterian Church (1822) in Camden, South Carolina. The church has an unusual feature: two pedimented porticoes, one on the front façade as well as one on the back. A two-stage tower and steeple rises from the roof at the rear of the church above a small pedimented portico that encloses a crisscrossed staircase; it balances the larger pedimented portico at the front. The interior reveals Mills's awareness of the increasing popularity of preachers at the start of the Second Great Awakening. Simple, with little decoration, the interior's sloped floor, coved ceiling, and raised pulpit all contribute to improved sightlines and acoustics.

THE RISE OF GOTHIC REVIVAL

Wealthy Episcopalians escaping the cold brought the Gothic Revival style to Florida. Supporting its use was John Freeman Young, the bishop of Florida, who had served as assistant rector of Trinity Church in New York City. Young was familiar with Upjohn's book, *Rural Architecture,* and may have brought it to Florida to help erect St. Mary's Episcopal Church (1878) in Green Cove Springs, Florida, a typical small board-and-batten Gothic Revival church.

The popularity of the Gothic Revival style and its association with Christian ideals continued to resonate

One of the best examples of the Carpenter Gothic style in Florida, St. Mary's Episcopal features a square steeple with an octangle spire. The church's original vessels for Holy Communion are still used in services today. St. Mary's Episcopal Church (1878), Green Cove Springs, Florida.

Construction on this Gothic Revival jewel took 83 years (1907–1990), and the results are dramatic: a soaring 301-foot central tower (the highest point in the District of Columbia), 215 stained glass windows, 110 gargoyle statues, and even more angels. The cathedral is the third-largest church in the United States and the sixth-largest church in the world. Cathedral Church of St. Peter and St. Paul (Washington National Cathedral) (started 1907), Washington, D.C.

with clergy and architects into the 20th century. In 1907, construction started on the Cathedral Church of St. Peter and St. Paul (Washington National Cathedral) in the U.S. capital. The structure is decorated with many Gothic motifs, including finials, carved bosses, gargoyles and grotesques, and stained glass windows.

ROMANESQUE REVIVAL AND PREACHING CONGREGATIONS

The South Atlantic region provides many impressive examples of the Romanesque Revival style, including Lovely Lane Methodist Church (1884) in Baltimore, Maryland. Designed by Stanford White, Lovely Lane was built to commemorate the centennial of Methodism in the United States as well as the city where Francis Asbury was ordained as the nation's first Methodist minister.

OPPOSITE: **Washington National Cathedral is not only neo-Gothic in design, but it is also built using an entire Gothic structural system of stone ribbed vaults and flying buttresses.** Cathedral Church of St. Peter and St. Paul.

RIGHT: **Known as the "mother church of American Methodism," Lovely Lane Methodist Church is modeled after historic churches from the 6th to 12th centuries. Its monumental bell tower is Italian Romanesque, while the dome covering its broad sanctuary is patterned after the 6th-century dome at Hagia Sophia in Istanbul, Turkey.** Lovely Lane Methodist Church (1884), Baltimore, Maryland.

OPPOSITE: **After the original structure was destroyed in a fire in 1861, a new Circular Congregational Church was built in the Romanesque Revival style. Inspired by Henry Hobson Richardson's design of Trinity Church in Boston, Massachusetts, the new structure features similar round arched windows on the façade, heavy massive walls, and a large lantern-shape tower over the nave.** Circular Congregational Church (1890), Charleston, South Carolina.

Another interpretation of Romanesque Revival is the Circular Congregational Church (1890) in Charleston, South Carolina. Its name harkens back to the congregation's earlier church designed by Robert Mills, which had a large circular space covered with a dome. (The building was destroyed in a fire in 1861.)

THE MODERN ERA

Perhaps the nation's most innovative architect was Frank Lloyd Wright. In 1941 he was asked to design the entire campus of Florida Southern College at Lakeland, Florida, including the Annie Pfeiffer Memorial Chapel. Lacking any overt religious symbolism, the building's interior is an auditorium with raked seating and a balcony sweeping around it. The only indication of its function is the chancel and pulpit. Skylights provide natural illumination.

STAINED GLASS

One common misconception about stained glass is that all the windows are made in the medieval technique of bits of colored glass held together by lead veins to form pictures. In the 19th century, artists began to paint on glass because it was cheaper and more efficient than the earlier method. New technologies have also been introduced, most famously the opalescent glass developed in the late 19th century by Louis Comfort Tiffany and John La Farge.

As increasingly larger windows were being installed in churches in the 12th century, French priest Abbot Suger of the Abbey of St. Denis outside of Paris introduced the use of stained glass. His purpose was to incorporate into the windows' designs biblical imagery and symbols that could be used to educate illiterate worshipers. Another purpose was more conceptual: He viewed the light filtering through the colored glass as spiritual light that transformed the church's interior into sacred space. The practice quickly spread throughout Europe but came to a halt with the onset of the Renaissance in the 16th century. Practical reasons prevailed as well: Worshipers were becoming more literate and needed natural light in order to read their prayer books and see the preacher.

The 19th-century Romantic Movement coupled with the Second Great Awakening rekindled interest in stained glass. As its popularity increased, even Georgian and Federal churches embraced stained glass, such as Trinity Episcopal Church (1726) in Newport, Rhode Island, which had its clear glass windows replaced with stained glass, including two made in the famed studios of Louis Comfort Tiffany. John La Farge also designed many highly regarded stained glass windows, including those installed in Trinity Church, Boston (see photo, right). Not all stained glass is figurative, however. One of the craft's most famous designers was Frank Lloyd Wright, who not only designed stained glass windows for his famous prairie-style homes but also for Unity Temple in Oak Park, Illinois.

Stained glass went into a second decline during the Great Depression in the 1930s but experienced a revival following World War II. It continues to be popular, as seen in the magnificent stained glass windows installed in the Cathedral of St. Joseph (dedicated 1962) in Hartford, Connecticut.

Frank Lloyd Wright's modern design of Annie Pfeiffer Memorial Chapel is complex; only a hexagonal tower on the exterior provides a visual clue as to what the rectangular building below it might be. Annie Pfeiffer Memorial Chapel (1941), Lakeland, Florida.

CHAPTER FOUR

NORTH CENTRAL REGION

In 1671, in what is now Michigan, a Jesuit priest proclaimed the Mississippi River and the Great Lakes region to be possessions of France. Evidence of French occupation remains in the names of some of this region's major cities, such as Detroit, Michigan, and St. Louis, Missouri. In 1763, the British gained possession following the French and Indian Wars, but their control was short-lived. Two major events shaped the region following America's War for Independence: The Northwest Territory, formed by Congress in 1787, encompassed the area that became the states bordering the Great Lakes, and the Louisiana Purchase, concluded in 1803, opened the vast territory west of the Mississippi River. Within a relatively short period, an entire continent was opened for settlement. The indigenous people were slowly and painfully pushed westward as pioneers hungry for land and a new beginning arrived.

OPPOSITE: **In the shadows of the Gateway Arch, the Basilica of St. Louis, the King of France, was the first cathedral west of the Mississippi. The surrounding land became part of the Jefferson National Expansion Memorial in 1933, and the basilica was the only area building of its era not to be razed.** Basilica of St. Louis, the King of France (Old Cathedral) (1834), St. Louis, Missouri.

THE FRENCH CONNECTION

Father Jacques Marquette and Louis Jolliet established missions along the North Central region's waterways, including Holy Family in 1699. Located at Cahokia, Illinois, this parish remained in French hands until the end of the French and Indian Wars in 1763, when France ceded most of its territory in the New World to the British. A second church, Holy Family Catholic Church, was dedicated at the site in 1799 and is now the oldest active Catholic parish in the United States.

A far cry from the simplicity of Holy Family is a cathedral erected in the region by descendants of early French settlers. The Basilica of St. Louis, the King of France (Old Cathedral) (1834) in St. Louis, Missouri, exhibits Federal-style features, including a pedimented portico. Only the cathedral's lavish interior reveals its worshipers' faith.

An early example of French vertical log construction, Holy Family Catholic Church represented the beauty of holiness to those living in an untamed wilderness. Holy Family Catholic Church (dedicated 1799), Cahokia, Illinois.

THE UTOPIANS

Among the North Central region's first settlers were Utopians who were intent upon forming ideal societies away from the temptations of the materialistic world. Shakers establishing societies in Ohio and Indiana made Union Village, a town near Cincinnati, the headquarters of the Shaker bishopric in the West from 1805 to 1912. German Lutheran Separatists migrating from Pennsylvania under the leadership of George Rapp purchased 30,000 acres in Indiana's Wabash River Valley in 1814 for a commune they named Harmony (later called New Harmony). It was successful, but Rapp,

Contrary to its name, The Roofless Church is all roof—an open-air shingled canopy that cloaks a quiet place for meditation. The Roofless Church (1960), New Harmony, Indiana.

The first temple built by the Mormon church under the auspices of Joseph Smith, Jr., the Kirtland Temple consists of native Ohio sandstone and lumber in its design. The structure features elements of Federal, Greek Revival, and Gothic Revival architecture. Kirtland Temple (dedicated 1836), Kirtland, Ohio.

fearing its members were becoming too materialistic, sold it to Robert Owen, a Welsh industrialist who transformed it into a secular society devoted to social reform.

New Harmony was all but abandoned in 1827, but in the 1950s, one of Owen's descendants, Kenneth Owen, and his wife, Jane, began to restore and revitalize it. They invited Philip Johnson to design a church that would provide a spiritual oasis for people of all faiths. The Roofless Church (1960) achieves this goal. Entrance into the church's grounds is through gates designed by Jacques Lipchitz, who also created the sculpture "The Descent of the Holy Spirit" that stands under the canopy.

Mormons forced to flee Palmyra, New York, because of their religious beliefs arrived in Kirtland, Ohio, in 1831. It was here that their leader, Joseph Smith, Jr., received a revelation that included detailed instructions on how to erect a temple. The eclectic style of Kirtland Temple (dedicated 1836) incorporates elements from Federal, Greek Revival, and even Gothic Revival movements. The temple's interior arrangement is particularly unique. The building has two courts: a lower level for the sacrament offerings, preaching, and praying, and an upper level for a school for apostles and priesthood meetings.

Following the murder of Joseph Smith, Jr., in 1844, his son Joseph III founded the Reorganized Church of Jesus Christ of Latter Day Saints, now the Community of Christ. Its contemporary temple and headquarters is centered on the twisting 300-foot stainless-steel spire jutting from the dome below. Community of Christ Temple and Auditorium (1994), Independence, Missouri.

Soon after the temple's dedication, the Mormons were once again forced to flee, this time settling on the banks of the Mississippi River where they founded the city of Nauvoo, Illinois, in 1839. Again facing persecution, the Mormons witnessed the murder of Smith and his brother Hiram in 1844. Disputes that followed resulted in the Mormons splitting into two groups. One followed Brigham Young westward to Utah, while the other, under the leadership of Joseph Smith III, established the Reorganized Church of Jesus Christ of Latter Day Saints. Recently renamed Community of Christ, its world headquarters houses a temple and administrative offices. The building's most distinctive feature is a spiraling form that rises skyward 300 feet.

FEDERAL STYLE MOVES WEST

Until 1840, Connecticut laid claim to the area known as Western Reserve, which centered on Cleveland, Ohio. Yankees moving into the area began to build churches similar to the ones they left behind back East, including Atwater Congregational Church (1838–41) in Atwater, Ohio. The structure's pedimented portico and tower are indeed Federal, but the pointed arch windows reveal its designer's awareness of the emerging Gothic Revival style in the East.

It wasn't just Yankees who were attracted to the Federal style's classical precedents. German Catholics who settled in Cincinnati, Ohio, and wanted to make a dramatic statement about their presence in the city chose to erect a church that would outdo those being built by their Protestant neighbors. However, unlike the Basilica of St. Louis that borrows features from classical architectural sources, St. Peter in Chains Roman Catholic Cathedral (1845) is modeled after an actual Greek temple—Temple of the Winds. The monumental structure also features a typical Wren/Gibbs tower and steeple.

A Greek Revival departure from the classical norm, St. Peter in Chains features a unique limestone steeple, rising 221 feet into the air. The ornate Corinthian columns on its exterior portico impart an aura of strength. St. Peter in Chains Roman Catholic Cathedral (1845), Cincinnati, Ohio.

FAR LEFT: **Featuring elements of both Federal and Gothic Revival styles, Atwater Congregational Church near Cleveland was among the first churches erected by Easterners moving west.** Atwater Congregational Church (1838–41), Atwater, Ohio.

LAND, IMMIGRANTS, AND CHURCHES

The Homestead Act of 1862, which offered 160 acres of free land to anyone who would work it for five years, attracted thousands of immigrants from land-starved Europe. Often entire communities or congregations would emigrate.

One of the first tasks addressed by many of these communities was to build a church in which they could carry on their traditions. These religious structures were often eclectic in style, borrowing features from a variety of sources.

Dutch Reformed Christians settled in Michigan and named their community Holland, famous today for its Tulip Festival. The Third Reformed Church (1874), the congregation's third building, was designed and built by a Dutch carpenter who learned his craft by studying pattern and planning books. The church's outstanding feature is its corner tower with a spire that rises 125 feet.

The interior of the Third Reformed Church prior to the installation of a pipe organ in the early 1980s is marked by lofty arches, Gothic-inspired light fixtures, and elaborate stained glass windows. Third Reformed Church (1874), Holland, Michigan.

Built by Swedish immigrants who took advantage of the Homestead Act, Cross of Christ Lutheran Church in Minnesota serves as an excellent example of the Gothic Revival style in the North Central region. Cross of Christ Lutheran Church (1878), Goodhue County, Minnesota.

Scandinavian and German Lutherans often chose to erect churches that had Gothic features similar to those found in the religious architecture of their homelands. These small white clapboard structures usually feature a large entry tower surmounted by a steeple and pointed-arched windows and doorways. They have become as much an American icon as the New England Federal-style church on the village green.

YANKEES AND THE SPREAD OF GOTHIC REVIVAL

Considered more "Christian" than Federal or Greek Revival, the Gothic Revival style gained in popularity in rural areas with the publication of Richard Upjohn's book, *Rural Architecture,* in 1852. Brought west by Episcopal missionaries, the book was used by carpenters to construct small wooden churches, thus the style's name "Carpenter Gothic."

As this style gained in popularity, it was adopted by various denominations, including the Congregationalists. They built First Congregational Church of Bradford (1864) near Nashua, Iowa, made famous as "The Little Brown Church in the Vale" in the song "The Church in the Wildwood" by William S. Pitts. While Gothic Revival on the exterior, its austere interior features a pulpit in place of an altar—typical of Congregational meetinghouses.

FAR RIGHT: **Built after the Great Chicago Fire in 1871, the Second Presbyterian's Gothic Revival design was the handiwork of James Renwick, the architect behind St. Patrick's Cathedral in New York City.** Second Presbyterian Church (1872–74; interior 1900–01), Chicago, Illinois.

This quaint Congregational church was popularized in the song "The Church in the Wildwood." The original paint job was the result of a tight budget: Long-lasting (albeit drab brown) Ohio Mineral Paint was the least expensive paint its strapped founders could find. First Congregational Church of Bradford (1864), Nashua, Iowa.

The influence of Trinity Episcopal Church and St. Patrick's Cathedral in New York City resulted in monumental Gothic Revival churches being built in all of the North Central region's major cities. James Renwick, the architect responsible for the design of New York's St. Patrick's Cathedral, designed the Second Presbyterian Church (1872–74; interior 1900–01) in Chicago. The monumental church is modeled after 15th-century

English Gothic churches. After a fire devastated much of the church in 1900, Chicago architect Howard Van Doren Shaw transformed the church's interior into the English Arts and Crafts style. The structure is famous for its stained glass windows; 14 of them are by Louis Comfort Tiffany or were created in his studios, including the "Jeweled Window," which received its name from its thousands of tiny, irregularly chipped and faceted pieces of glass, each separately leaded.

INDUSTRY, IMMIGRANTS, AND CHURCHES

Many of the laborers in the North Central region's growing industries were recruited from impoverished areas of eastern and southern Europe. Of these, a significant number were Roman Catholics who settled in ethnic neighborhoods in large crowded cities. Although poorly paid and often living in squalid conditions, these immigrants felt it was important to erect churches where they could worship, speak in their native tongue, and maintain age-old traditions. Their churches, often monumental in size and elaborate in appearance, were an oasis of beauty and tranquility for their members. The styles of the structures varied depending upon the appearance of the churches left behind in the Old Country.

This was the case for Polish immigrants. They preferred the elaborate interpretations of the Renaissance or Baroque styles found in their homeland even though these types of churches were costly to build. A magnificent example is St. Mary of Perpetual Help (1889–92) in the Bridgeport neighborhood of Chicago. Established in 1886 as a parish for Polish immigrants working in meatpacking plants, the church's elaborate façade includes a large central dome and flanking towers. The interior is equally overwhelming, with successive domes that lead to a chancel decorated with paintings of Polish saints.

The Beaux-Arts style was introduced at the World's Columbian Exposition in Chicago in 1893, and from there it spread throughout the North Central region. Roman Catholic parishes that were ethnically mixed

Immigrant communities often built churches that were reminiscent of the churches they left behind in Europe. One example, Mary Queen of the World (1870–94) in Montréal was modeled after St. Peter's in Rome and was built over the course of nearly 25 years in the late 19th century. The Baroque stone façade is capped with several copper domes and ornate sculptures of patron saints. Mary Queen of the World (1870–94), Montréal, Québec, Canada.

The dramatic Baroque architecture of this Roman Catholic church in Chicago's Bridgeport neighborhood is a nod to the churches its initial parishioners, mainly Polish immigrants, left behind in the Old World. St. Mary of Perpetual Help (1889–92), Chicago, Illinois.

A classical Renaissance gem, the Cathedral of St. Paul is the cross-town counterpart to the Basilica of St. Mary in Minneapolis (see pages 28 and 79). The cathedral's exterior is made from Minnesota-quarried granite. Cathedral of St. Paul (1906–15), St. Paul, Minnesota.

often preferred this style because it was viewed as lacking any specific national identity. Emmanuel Masqueray, a L'école des Beaux-Arts–trained French architect, designed the Basilica of St. Mary (started 1907) in Minneapolis as well as its contemporary, the Cathedral of St. Paul. For both, the architect used classical detailing and proportion.

Like most Roman Catholic immigrants, Orthodox Christians living in urban areas selected plans and styles that were dependent upon the traditional ones found in their homelands. Many of their churches were monumental, while other parishes chose more modest design models.

The distinctive Holy Trinity Orthodox Cathedral is characteristic of Christian Orthodox churches of the early 20th century, marked by its onion domes and Orthodox crosses. Holy Trinity Orthodox Cathedral (1899–1903), Chicago, Illinois.

The wide nave of the Basilica of St. Mary culminates in the sanctuary, which is surrounded by an iron grill and an entablature supporting statues of the 12 apostles. In the center of the sanctuary, a 40-foot marble *baldacchino* covers the original altar. Basilica of St. Mary (started 1907), Minneapolis, Minnesota.

The congregants of Holy Trinity Orthodox Cathedral (1899–1903) hired Louis Sullivan, one of Chicago's most prominent architects, to design a structure reminiscent of the intimate, rural buildings they left behind in Russia. The result is a small, elegant church capped with onion domes that would look at home in the rural Carpathian Mountains of southern Russia. Holy Trinity is similar to the churches Orthodox Christians erected in small towns and rural areas.

PREACHING CONGREGATIONS AND ROMANESQUE REVIVAL

Churches built by preaching congregations who favored the Romanesque Revival style can be found in many of the North Central region's cities. One outstanding example, Wesley Methodist in Minneapolis, Minnesota (see page 23), was designed by architect Warren H. Hayes and built in the 1890s. The church features an auditorium plan with raked seating and a curved balcony

Built by Discalced Carmelite Friars as a pilgrimage site, Holy Hill's location and Romanesque Revival style are reminiscent of the German homeland many Wisconsin settlers left behind. Holy Hill (the National Shrine of Mary, Help of Christians) (started 1926), near Milwaukee, Wisconsin.

covered by a shallow dome filled with stained glass. Wesley Methodist retains its side doors that rise up to allow people seated in the adjoining Sunday school wing to hear the preacher.

SHRINES, GROTTOS, AND CHAPELS

Holy Hill (the National Shrine of Mary, Help of Christians) (started 1926) sits high atop a hill west of Milwaukee. Designed in the Romanesque Revival style, the church's grounds include a pathway lined with life-size statues depicting the 14 stations of the cross.

Holy Hill is dramatically situated, but much of this region is covered by flat prairie. One way to relieve the tedium of the landscape is to imbue it with the extraordinary. Working alone or aided by parishioners, priests, often in response to a religious vow, would build elaborate stone and concrete grottos decorated with colored glass, broken ceramics, semiprecious gems, shells, and other found objects that are glorious expressions of folk art and spirituality. One outstanding example is Dickeyville Grotto (1925–30) in Dickeyville, Wisconsin, on the grounds of Holy Ghost Parish and built by Father Mathias Wernerus.

To create this folk-art masterpiece, concrete was modeled around metal forms or poured into slabs. Then bits of glass, tiles, crockery, stone, shells, costume jewelry, and other materials were pressed into the concrete. Dickeyville Grotto (1925–30), Dickeyville, Wisconsin.

MODERNITY AND CHURCH ARCHITECTURE

Maybe the idea of the frontier as a place for new beginnings contributed to the North Central region being home to so many architectural innovations. Freed of the conventions of the past, architects imagined and then created the future. For example, the nation's first skyscrapers were built in Chicago, and Unity Temple (1906)—often considered the most unique church of any time—was built not far from the city in Oak Park, Illinois. Designed by Frank Lloyd Wright, the structure was the forerunner of numerous innovative churches in the North Central region.

An apprentice of Wright, Francis Barry Byrne designed a church that has been called the first modern American Catholic Church. The exterior of St. Thomas the Apostle Church (1924) in Chicago has been described as a reinterpretation of Gothic mixed with Art Nouveau or as a modern evocation of a Spanish mission church. Regardless of its style, it is the church's interior that is most unusual for its time. Rather than

Although it was built almost a century ago, Frank Lloyd Wright's Unity Temple deservedly enjoys a reputation as one of its architect's true masterworks. The cubical, reinforced concrete structure remains one of the boldest departures from architectural tradition in the United States, religious or secular. Unity Temple (1906), Oak Park, Illinois.

THE SECOND VATICAN COUNCIL

Liturgical reform among liberal Catholics was already under way in many quarters when Pope John XXIII convened the Second Vatican Council in 1962. The Council's goal was to recommend a pastoral course for the Catholic Church to follow in the 21st century. The Bishops met for three years. In 1963, Pope Paul VI promulgated their first document, *Sacrosanctum Concilium,* or the Constitution on the Sacred Liturgy. It urged Roman Catholics to discard their concepts of "triumphalism" when it came to designing and decorating their churches and to return to the communal practice of the early church by making the liturgy more accessible to the people. Mass was to be in the vernacular language, not Latin, and worship was to be the act of the entire congregation in concert with clergy. As a result of this document, older Roman Catholic churches have been reconfigured to bring the altar closer to the people, and their interiors have been stripped of much of their art and artifacts.

FAR RIGHT: **A modern reinterpretation of a Spanish mission, St. Thomas the Apostle Church has been called "the first modern Catholic church building." Architect Barry Byrne described terra cotta sculptor Alfonso Ianelli as his creative equal in designing the ornate fortresslike façade.** St. Thomas the Apostle Church (1924), Chicago, Illinois.

Softly lit by natural light filtering in from side windows, the interior of First Christian Church is as unadorned as its exterior. First Christian Church (1942), Columbus, Indiana.

the conventional basilica plan favored for liturgical churches prior to Vatican II, the nave of this church is almost as broad as it is long. Since the roof is unsupported by arches or pillars, all parishioners have a clear view of the altar in the sanctuary that juts out into the nave.

Members of First Christian Church (1942) in Columbus, Indiana, asked the Finnish architect Eliel Saarinen to design an unadorned church that would express their theology based on Christian fundamentals but would also be beautiful. The result is an austere brick rectangular church; its only decoration on the exterior is a large cross set against limestone placed in a grid pattern (see page 32). The design's only concession to the past is a tall attached bell tower.

CHAPTER FIVE

SOUTH CENTRAL REGION

Spain and France originally controlled the southern part of America's South Central region, and their cultures have left their marks, particularly in Louisiana and Texas. By 1803, these two countries had ceded most of the land they possessed to the United States, opening up millions of acres of rich land for settlement. People from Virginia, Maryland, and the Carolinas began arriving in the South Central region, including tobacco growers, who introduced the plantation culture to the area, and Scotch-Irish and German pioneers, who established small subsistence farms. In 1817, Oklahoma Territory became home to displaced North American Indians; all others were forbidden by law from settling there. As the demand for more land increased, the government relented, and "land runs" in 1889 and 1893 resulted in the entry of thousands of homesteaders. The Civil War also had a major impact on this area, disrupting its economy and discouraging settlement. Church construction all but ceased until a decade following the war's conclusion.

Originally a rest stop of sorts on El Camino Real (King's Highway), La Iglesia de Mission San Jose y San Miguel de Aguayo was once a compound with a population of 350. Another former Spanish mission, the Alamo, is just across town. La Iglesia de Mission San Jose y San Miguel de Aguayo (1768), San Antonio, Texas.

SPAIN AND FRANCE

To cement its foothold in southern Texas, Spain began to establish missions along the San Antonio River and in the lower Rio Grande Valley. La Iglesia dė Mission San Jose y San Miguel de Aguayo (1768) is one of several missions in San Antonio. The façade of the church, constructed of thick stone walls, is distinguished by a square bell tower and rich decoration, particularly around its main entrance. Niches hold statues of saints, all identified by their attributes; religious symbols include the Sacred Heart of Jesus encircled with thorns.

France established colonies along the Gulf Coast, founding the seaport towns of Mobile, Alabama, and New Orleans, Louisiana. In laying out both cities, the French left space in a prominent location for a Catholic church. In 1822, an Episcopal church replaced the Catholic church in Mobile, but one still stands on the site in New Orleans.

Shells, scrolls, flowers, and other decorative motifs abound on the exterior of La Iglesia de Mission San Jose y San Miguel de Aguayo, yet the interior is relatively unadorned. Its outstanding features include a barrel vault spanning the nave and a dome covering the crossing. La Iglesia de Mission San Jose y San Miguel de Aguayo.

St. Louis Cathedral on Jackson Square has a complicated history. Spaniard Don Andres Almonester y Roxas financed its construction in 1794; in 1820 and again in 1851, the cathedral underwent considerable remodeling, which left little of the original structure. As a result, its style defies classification, incorporating details from a variety of sources, including neoclassical. St. Louis Cathedral (1794, 1820, 1851), New Orleans, Louisiana.

MISSIONARIES AND PIONEERS

The "Trail of Tears" that the Choctaw Indians were forced to follow from their homes in Mississippi ended in Oklahoma. Missionaries accompanied them, including the Reverend Alfred Wright, who founded the Wheelock Mission Presbyterian Church (1846) in McCurtain County, Oklahoma. Vaguely Greek Revival in style, the church is built of local stone, hand chiseled into shape, and is topped by a wooden steeple over its front entrance. The building was badly damaged by a fire in 1866 but has been restored to its original appearance. It is now Oklahoma's oldest church and stands as a memorial to Reverend Wright and his missionary efforts among Native Americans.

Roman Catholic pioneers moving west from Maryland settled Bardstown, Kentucky, in the 1770s. By 1808, its Catholic community had grown so large it was named one of four American Roman Catholic Sees, the first west of the Allegheny Mountains. The town's small brick church was soon replaced by a far more magnificent

Founded after the forced migration of the Choctaw tribe (now known as the "Trail of Tears"), Wheelock Mission Presbyterian Church was rebuilt in the 1880s after the original was razed in a Civil War–era fire. Wheelock Mission Presbyterian Church (1846), McCurtain County, Oklahoma.

Except for niches on its façade that hold sculptural images of saints, the red brick St. Joseph Proto-Cathedral, with its gleaming white pedimented portico and steeple, is modeled after Federal-style churches in the East.
St. Joseph Proto-Cathedral (1819), Bardstown, Kentucky.

structure, St. Joseph Proto-Cathedral (1819). Parish members contributed money as well as material and labor toward the cathedral's construction.

PROSPERITY AND THE GREEK REVIVAL STYLE

Protestant denominations whose worship services focused on the words of the preacher comprised a large proportion of the South Central region's first settlers. At about this same time the Greek Revival style began to sweep the nation. The style had great appeal to these settlers, not only for its democratic symbolism but also because of its lack of Catholic overtones. Its expansive uncluttered interior space allowed the congregation to gather close to the preacher.

Small versions of the Greek Revival style can be found throughout the South Central region's rural areas. Plantation owners erected Kingston Methodist Church (1856–57) outside of Natchez, Mississippi. The elegant church's stucco walls, scored to look like stone blocks, along with its entrance portico supported by two large columns and surmounted by a pediment, contribute to its templelike appearance.

An example of Greek Revival architecture in the rural South, Kingston Methodist Church was built by plantation owners a few years before the start of the Civil War. The structure is southeast of the town of Natchez. Kingston Methodist Church (1856–57), near Natchez, Mississippi.

Architect James Cook designed this exemplary Carpenter Gothic board-and-batten house of worship. Iuka citizens bought the church from the Episcopal Diocese in the 1980s, and it later won awards for its painstaking restoration. Church of Our Saviour, Episcopal (1873), Iuka, Mississippi.

EPISCOPALIANS AND THE GOTHIC REVIVAL

Religious revivalism brought an end to the popularity of the Greek Revival style, and in moved Gothic architecture, which was considered more authentic for Christians. Plantation owners moving west from Virginia introduced the Gothic Revival style to the South. Only a handful of the thousands of small Carpenter Gothic frame churches built at this time survive. The collapse of the plantation system following the Civil War resulted in many Episcopalians moving away from rural areas. Their small frame board-and-batten churches were abandoned, and many were demolished. Many of those that did survive are maintained by preservation societies. The fine crafting evident in St. Andrew's Episcopal Church (1853–54) in Prairieville, Alabama, is a testimony to the skill of the

CHURCH PRESERVATION

Churches are important as places of worship and community centers, but they are also repositories of history, often the only primary evidence remaining of a community. Unfortunately, many of North America's historic churches have been lost, either to a wrecking ball, abandonment, or thoughtless remodeling. An inscription on a tombstone in the cemetery of a small rural Methodist church in Minnesota reads: "Look ye on high and believe I am there. When I am gone I am gone." The epitaph refers to the fate of one person, but it also recalls the fate of many historic places of worship—once they are gone they are lost forever. While the loss of a building cannot be equated to the loss of life, houses of worship, often more than any other type of building, are embodiments of people's lives—of its members' life cycles and of their highest aspirations.

Preservationists recognize that not every building can be saved and that the preservation is not a simple task. But efforts like those in Mississippi, where the Church of Our Saviour (see above) was preserved, must be made to ensure that historically or aesthetically important structures are not lost. This is a particularly difficult task with religious properties. The First Amendment to the U.S. Constitution, which guarantees the freedom to worship, also prevents the government from interfering in the fate of religious buildings. This separation of church and state has contributed to the loss of many historic religious properties.

slaves who built it. The design of Church of Our Saviour, Episcopal (1873) in Iuka, Mississippi, is credited to English-born architect James Cook, although its style reveals his familiarity with Richard Upjohn's book.

Gothic Revival had widespread appeal, especially to immigrants who were familiar with the style in their homelands. German and Czech Catholics who settled in Texas built and decorated their churches to replicate ones left behind in their homelands. One of the most completely realized is The Nativity of Mary, Blessed Virgin Roman Catholic Church (1906) in High Hill, Texas. The third church erected on the site, the structure is partly constructed of material from the second wooden structure, including 18 stained glass windows. Its interior is elaborately decorated with sculpture, faux marble columns and altar, and most famously, the paintings that cover its walls and ribbed vault ceiling. This church as well as others with such decorated interiors are called the "Painted Churches of Texas" and are popular tourist attractions.

OPPOSITE: **Erected a decade before the Civil War, St. Andrew's is a testament to the superb crafting of the slaves who built it. The red Carpenter Gothic church was constructed according to mass-produced blueprints by renowned architect Richard Upjohn that served as the basis for thousands of rural southern churches.** St. Andrew's Episcopal Church (1853–54), Prairieville,

Ferdinand Stockert and Hermann Kern guided the vividly realized interior of the Nativity of Mary in 1912. The church is known as one of the "Painted Churches of Texas" because of the lavish painting inside, which was designed to interplay with the shadows. The Nativity of Mary, Blessed Virgin Roman Catholic Church (1906), High Hill, Texas.

With its two towers and triple arcaded entrance, this Romanesque Revival structure is known for more than its architecture: On September 15, 1963, in the midst of the Civil Rights struggle, a bomb exploded near the sanctuary, taking the lives of four little girls. 16th Street Baptist Church (1909–11), Birmingham, Alabama.

THE ROMANESQUE REVIVAL

As mentioned in previous chapters, the Gothic Revival style did not appeal to many Protestant congregations. They preferred the Romanesque style, with its massive walls and militant appearance; however, the traditional basilica plan was replaced with an expansive auditorium. In the South, this style and plan were particularly appealing to African-American congregations, with their tradition of dynamic preachers and large choirs.

A pioneering African-American architect in Alabama, Wallace A. Rayfield (1874–1941) designed one of America's most famous churches in this style—16th Street Baptist Church (1909–11) in Birmingham. Today, the church is part of a larger complex that includes the Birmingham Civil Rights Institute (1992), designed by the African-American architectural firms Bond Ryder James of New York City and Robert L. Brown Associates of Decatur, Georgia.

MODERNITY AND CHURCH ARCHITECTURE

With all its references to democratic values and American ideals, the Federal style experienced a rebirth following World War II. Church congregations who longed for the time when religion played an important role in people's lives particularly favored the style. The Perkins Chapel (1951) at Southern Methodist University in Dallas, Texas, is one example of a religious structure designed to impress students with America's Christian values.

More common in the latter part of the 20th century was the effort by architects and their clients to find a new vocabulary to express ancient Christian values. No longer were towers, spires, and domes acceptable; those represented the past. Another structural feature had to be found to express a spiritual quest. For a period it was huge roofs reaching upward from ground level toward the heavens. Then the trend became just the opposite—the appearance of no roof at all.

An excellent example of this trend is the Tuskegee Chapel (1968–69) in Alabama. Used as a concert hall for the famed Tuskegee University choir, its roof is all but invisible. Instead, the chapel has massive, curved asymmetrical brick walls that cause the building to look different from every angle. One wall rises upward, reminiscent of a tower, and a cross at the rear

Located on the Dallas campus of Southern Methodist University, Perkins Chapel features architecture reminiscent of the neoclassical style originated by Sir Christopher Wren. The brick and stone church is capped with a zinc-plated steeple and gilded cross. Perkins Chapel (1951), Dallas, Texas.

Home of the renowned Tuskegee University choir, the striking Tuskegee Chapel has equally renowned architecture. The acoustically innovative structure has nary a right angle. Tuskegee Chapel (1968–69), Tuskegee University, Alabama.

over the chapel assures its identity. The interior consists of a fan-shape auditorium with a large choir and pulpit that juts out into the congregation.

Another unique example of modern architecture in this region is set in the midst of a forest in the Ozark Mountains. The intimate nondenominational Thorncrown Chapel (1980) in Eureka Springs, Arkansas, was designed by E. Fay Jones, a former apprentice of Frank Lloyd Wright. Its harmony with nature evokes Wright's organic modernism, yet its deceptive simplicity is more remindful of another great architect, Mies van der Rohe.

POSTMODERNISM IN THE SOUTH

In recent years, the South has become a destination for northerners seeking a more hospitable climate in a less crowded environment. The increase in population is

FAR RIGHT: **Built almost entirely of 2×4-foot pine studs that frame its glass walls, the tall, narrow Thorncrown Chapel appears to emerge out of its environment, surrounding worshipers with the beauty of holiness found within nature.** Thorncrown Chapel (1980), Eureka Springs, Arkansas.

evident in the numerous churches that have recently been erected in the region. St. Thomas More Catholic Church (1996) in Paducah, Kentucky, was built for a growing parish. In the postmodern spirit, its architecture reflects the Catholic Church's past and the parish's present needs. The church complex consists of a series of buildings linked by a covered ambulatory intended to recall those found at European monasteries. A large, square, brick bell tower, a spare version of medieval towers found in Italy, serves to identify the building from a distance. The interior is designed to accommodate modern liturgical practices. Its broad auditorium-plan nave is arranged so there is seating on three sides of the altar. Natural light enters through large windows set behind the chancel and in the clerestory. The only religious imagery is a crucifix set behind the altar table.

In the realm of religious architecture, Philip Johnson is best known for his design of the Crystal Cathedral in

A 21st-century Catholic church, St. Thomas More has been described as a "simple, noble, stately building." The heavily windowed wall marks the modern architecture, while the commanding bell tower harkens back to convention. St. Thomas More Catholic Church (1996), Paducah, Kentucky.

Garden Grove, California—considered the first "megachurch" (see pages 24–25 and 124). Less well-known but perhaps more dramatic in appearance is the Chapel of St. Basil (1996–97) on the campus of the University of St. Thomas, Houston, Texas. It represents Johnson's interpretation of postmodernism. The elegant chapel's form echoes earlier Eastern Orthodox churches, including a gold dome topped with a cross. To proclaim its postmodernity, Johnson bisects the dome with an abstract granite sculptural plane.

Featuring dynamic lines, inspiring views, and a stark altar, the interior of St. Thomas More balances tradition with the modern demands of a growing parish. St. Thomas More Catholic Church.

A futuristic masterstroke by Philip Johnson—the architect behind the Crystal Cathedral in Garden Grove, California—the starkly postmodern Chapel of St. Basil represents another remarkable departure from tradition. The dome, gilded with 23.5-karat gold leaf, is connected to the cubical church body by a bisecting granite plane. Chapel of St. Basil (1996–97), Houston, Texas.

CHAPTER SIX

MOUNTAIN REGION

Comprising nearly one-third of the nation's land mass, this vast region can be divided culturally and geographically into two distinct areas: the Southwest, consisting of Arizona, New Mexico, and the southern portion of Colorado; and the West, which includes Nevada, Utah, Idaho, Wyoming, Montana, and northern Colorado. The first Europeans in the Southwest were Spanish explorers and Roman Catholic missionaries. The distinctive Mexican, Spanish, and Native American culture that developed in the area started to change in the mid-19th century when precious metals were discovered. Soon hordes of easterners began to arrive, all intent on finding the gold that eluded the Spanish. The situation in the West was quite different. The mountains of northern Arizona and southern Utah formed a natural barrier, preventing Spain from venturing farther north. Except for nomadic Native American tribes in search of game and furs and a few missions established by French priests, this area was virtually unoccupied until the mid-19th century.

One of the most well-preserved churches of its vintage, the stately adobe exterior of the chapel of San Jose de Garcia, an 18th-century Franciscan mission, is a fine example of Spanish colonial style. San Jose de Garcia (1760–76), Las Trampas, New Mexico.

Three events changed the Mountain region's character: the passage of the Donation Land Act in 1850, giving free land to anyone willing to settle in Oregon; the start of the California Gold Rush; and the arrival of Mormons at the shores of the Great Salt Lake in 1847. Suddenly thousands of pioneers were making the difficult journey westward along the Oregon Trail. Vast acres of rangeland unsuitable for farming attracted ranchers who could ship their cattle to eastern markets via the railroads. Romanticized images of the West resonated with easterners seeking an escape from their crowded cities. Major metropolitan and recreational areas have since developed, but the Southwest and West still retain their distinct character.

SPAIN'S SEARCH FOR SOULS

Spanish explorers brought with them to the New World the Laws of the Indies, which stated that the principal aim of Spain's exploration was to convert the indigenous people to Roman Catholicism. Franciscan priests accompanied explorers north from Mexico into what is now New Mexico. By 1660, they had established nearly 50 Franciscan churches in the area; however, none of these survived. Others were built, and in 1776 there were about 30 churches in use. Of these, San Jose de Garcia (1760–76) in Las Trampas is considered the most perfectly preserved.

Using age-old building techniques and material (adobe), villagers erected the small mission churches in New Mexico. Other than their plans, these churches owe little to Spanish or Mexican models; they are more a form of folk art. Cruciform in plan, San Jose de Garcia retains its choir balcony over the entrance. The wooden belfries

A full set of painted altarpieces, or *santos*, were made specifically for San Jose de Garcia in the 18th and 19th centuries by *santeros*, craftspeople who create religious objects. San Jose de Garcia.

A colorful hybrid of Spanish and Native American styles, Santuario de Chimayo's interior is notable for its intricate altar screen reredos. The cross on the altar—and the sand it was found in—is said to have miraculous curative powers, attracting thousands of visitors during Holy Week. Santuario de Chimayo (1813–16), Chimayo, New Mexico.

atop the bell towers are modern replacements. Inside are a 19th-century pulpit, a latticed altar rail, and a choir loft rail—all hand carved. Today the church is a National Historic Site.

Also designated a National Historic Site, Santuario de Chimayo (1813–16) was originally built as a private chapel by Don Bernardo Abeyta on a site that had long been associated with a healing cult. Pilgrims come to the church,

FAR LEFT: **Known locally as "The Lourdes of America," this Spanish colonial adobe shrine is located on the hillside where a crucifix was unearthed in 1810. The cross mysteriously kept vanishing and reappearing on the hill where it was found, leading to a permanent structure that is now said to be the most-visited church in New Mexico.** Santuario de Chimayo.

particularly during Holy Week, to eat its "holy dirt" and to leave gifts of thanksgiving. The exterior of the church has undergone changes, including the addition of a pitched metal roof. The interior is lavishly adorned with painted altarpieces and *bultos.*

Jesuit priests founded the missions in Arizona but were subsequently expelled from the area in 1767 by the Spanish. Replacing them were Franciscan missionaries who were responsible for building one of the nation's most beautiful churches, San Xavier del Bac Mission Church (1772–97), outside of Tucson (see right and pages 6–7). Unlike the mission churches in New Mexico, this one is modeled after Spanish Baroque churches. Built of burnt brick covered with stucco, the entire exterior is painted a gleaming white, except for the rich decoration that frames its entrance. Cruciform in plan with two towers (one never completed), the church has seven domes: three covering the nave, one in each transept, one over the apse, and a high dome above the crossing.

FAR RIGHT: **Except for the walls of the nave, the interior of San Xavier del Bac is lavishly decorated in the Baroque style, including gilded stucco and plaster, faux marble, and statues of saints set in niches—fully clothed *bultos* and painted *santos.*** San Xavier del Bac Mission Church (1772–97), Tucson, Arizona.

The influence of the Spanish Baroque style can also be seen throughout Mexico, as seen in the Old Basilica at the Shrine of Our Lady of Guadalupe (1709) in Mexico City. Constructed on the site of a 16th-century church (and an earlier Aztec temple), the structure was active as a house of worship until the late 1970s. Earthquakes made the building unstable, and it was closed to the public when the New Basilica opened nearby. Old Basilica at the Shrine of Our Lady of Guadalupe (1709), Mexico City, Mexico.

JESUIT MISSIONS IN THE NORTH

In 1814, the Jesuits were allowed to return to the Mountain region, and they began to set up missions to serve the native people and French-Canadian fur traders.

A Belgian-born Jesuit priest, Pierre Jean DeSmet, established a mission in 1841 on the banks of the Bitter Root River in what is now Montana. The mission was temporarily abandoned, but it was reopened by Father Antonio Ravalli, a gifted Italian priest and craftsperson. He designed and supervised the construction of St. Mary's Mission (1866) in Stevensville, Montana. Built of logs taken from the old mission church, its façade is covered with clapboard and features an entrance tower topped with a belfry. Inside, Father Ravalli designed and built the altar that stands under an intricately carved alcove. He also carved the candleholders that flank the altar and fashioned an almost life-size figure of St. Ignatius out of plaster. In 1879, Father Ravalli drew up the plans and supervised the construction of an addition that doubled the size of the church.

Far different in appearance is the church Father Ravalli designed for the Coeur d'Alene Mission of the Sacred Heart (ca 1850). The oldest structure in Idaho, the log and adobe church was an attempt to re-create in the

St. Mary's Mission was the first European-American settlement in what is now Montana. Abandoned after its initial 1841 founding by Father Pierre DeSmet, the mission later reopened under the guidance of Father Antonio Ravalli, who also designed the pictured church. St. Mary's Mission (1866), Stevensville, Montana.

wilds of Idaho a church whose façade is reminiscent of the 16th-century mother church of the Jesuits in Rome—Il Gesu. The church's interior is also modeled after Italian art, including a beautiful carved wood ceiling decorated to simulate stucco.

MORMONS: TABERNACLES AND TEMPLES

On July 24, 1847, an ailing Brigham Young viewed the valley between the Wasatch Mountains and the Great Salt Lake and proclaimed, "This is the place." On that

Father Antonio Ravalli adapted local materials to techniques popular in his native country of Italy when he built the original Coeur d'Alene Mission of the Sacred Heart. The mission moved west in 1877; this site later became a state park, but it is still used on August 15 for the Feast of the Assumption. Coeur d'Alene Mission of the Sacred Heart (ca 1850), near Caldwell, Idaho.

site fewer than 2,000 Mormons set out to establish what became Salt Lake City, Utah. It has been said that Mormons might be in the West, but they are not entirely of it. This is evident in the architectural styles they selected for many of their sacred buildings.

Mormon tabernacles are congregational buildings that serve a stake, which is similar to a parish or diocese. English architect Miles Romney designed St. George Tabernacle (1863–76) in St. George, Utah. Constructed of local red sandstone blocks, the building's design reflects the architect's knowledge of the Federal-style architecture inspired by Wren/Gibbs and was popular back East.

The Salt Lake Temple (1853–93) is only open to communicants to receive sacred instructions and to prepare to meet God. Young selected the architect, Truman Angell, and contributed many ideas for the temple's design. Borrowing features from Romanesque and Gothic Revival architecture, the building's fortresslike appearance is symbolic as well as practical. It conveys the spiritual power of the faith, but it can also double as a citadel to protect its followers from attack.

THE GOTHIC REVIVAL MOVES WEST

Clergy and pioneers brought revival styles west. One of the earliest examples is a church that defies any specific stylistic category—the Cathedral of St. Francis of Assisi

A Mormon church in the Wren/Gibbs tradition commonly seen in New England, St. George Tabernacle features a tower with an imported British clock. The sandstone and limestone blocks used in its construction were quarried by hand. St. George Tabernacle (1863–76), St. George, Utah.

Located in the heart of Salt Lake City, this fortresslike Mormon temple is open only to communicants of the Church of Jesus Christ of Latter Day Saints. Brigham Young commissioned the temple's construction, but he did not live to see its completion—40 years after the first stone was laid in 1853. Salt Lake Temple (1853–93), Salt Lake City, Utah.

in Santa Fe, New Mexico. Although its cornerstone was laid in 1867, it was not actually completed until a century later. Built of locally quarried stone, the cathedral does not follow the style of the centuries-old New Mexico churches built by the Spanish and Native Americans. Rather its patron, Archbishop Jean-Baptiste Lamy, used architectural features from the past as a means to revitalize the area's Catholicism, which he thought had decayed along with its churches.

A more monumental example of the Gothic Revival style is St. Mary's in the Mountains Roman Catholic Church (1877) in Virginia City, Nevada, a town that gained a reputation for its wealth (it was home of the famed Comstock Lode) and rowdiness from articles that appeared in eastern papers. St. Mary's was erected to accommodate a congregation of more than 3,000—mainly Mexican, Italian, and Irish miners.

Two enormous Catholic cathedrals were erected in the Mountain region in the early 20th century. Both reveal the longevity and appeal of the Gothic Revival style, particularly among Roman Catholics. Helena, Montana, was a very wealthy city when the Cathedral of Saint Helena (1908–24) was constructed. The Helena Diocese numbered about 50,000, many of whom were

TOP LEFT: **Archbishop Lamy wanted to include classic features in the design of the Cathedral of St. Francis of Assisi. The result is round-arched windows typical of the Romanesque architecture found in his native France. The structure also exhibits several Gothic elements, including a large rose window on the façade similar to those decorating the 13th-century church in Assisi, Italy, dedicated to St. Francis.** Cathedral of St. Francis of Assisi (started 1867), Santa Fe, New Mexico.

BOTTOM LEFT: **Another church in New Mexico that illustrates Archbishop Lamy's success at introducing historic Christian features into local architecture is the recently restored San Rafael Roman Catholic Church. It is an adobe church built in the Gothic Revival style—an anomaly among rural churches in New Mexico.** San Rafael Roman Catholic Church (ca 1865), La Cueva, New Mexico.

wealthy mine owners, including one who contributed $100,000 toward the cathedral's construction. The architect, A. O. Von Herbulis, was trained in Europe and incorporated elements from some of his favorite Gothic churches, including the Cathedral in Cologne, Germany, and Amiens Cathedral in France. At 230 feet, the cathedral's twin towers are the tallest structures in Helena.

Perhaps even more ambitious was Bishop Lawrence Scanlan, who arrived in Salt Lake City as a missionary in 1873. At the time there were 95 Catholics in the entire valley. By 1891 that number had increased to 3,000, and a decision was made to erect a church, now the Cathedral of the Madeleine. The Gothic Revival–style superstructure was completed by 1909, but except for the pews, the interior remained unfinished. This changed with the arrival of Bishop Joseph S. Glass in 1917. Among other additions, he provided the interior with a spiritual quality in the form of light filtering through stained glass windows.

FAR RIGHT: **Marked by its twin 230-foot red-tiled towers striving skyward, the opulent Cathedral of St. Helena was built in large part with donations from wealthy mining barons. The Gothic Revival archetype is primarily Indiana limestone, a more durable substance than Montana sandstone.** Cathedral of Saint Helena (1908–24), Helena, Montana.

Once the Comstock Lode ran out, the population of Virginia City, Nevada, declined from 20,000 to 1,500. Buildings were abandoned or, like this church, were stripped of their valuable decorations. But even in its stripped-down condition, St. Mary's continues to serve the town's Catholic residents. St. Mary's in the Mountains Roman Catholic Church (1877), Virginia City, Nevada.

THE MODERN MOVEMENT

Modernity entered the Mountain region with a flourish, as seen in two spectacular structures erected in the 1950s and '60s. It is not only jet planes that soar at the Air Force Academy at Colorado Springs, Colorado; so too do the walls of the Air Force Academy Cadet Chapel (1956–63). Designed by Walter A. Netsch, Jr., the chapel has three separate worship spaces on two floors: The

Bishop Glass added a carved wooden reredos to the Cathedral of the Madeleine and covered the walls with mosaic, marble, and paintings. Recently, the cathedral has undergone a complete renovation and restoration that includes a new onyx and marble altar set on a platform at the crossing of the nave and transepts. Cathedral of the Madeleine (1909), Salt Lake City, Utah.

The 17 triangular tetrahedrons that form the outer shell of the Air Force Academy Cadet Chapel have been described as evoking the shape of the mountains, a person's hands pressed together in prayer, or a group of tepees. The spaces between them are filled with colored glass that fills the interior with luminosity similar to that achieved in Gothic cathedrals. Air Force Academy Cadet Chapel (1956–63), Colorado Springs, Colorado.

The Protestant Chapel in the Air Force Academy Cadet Chapel is marked by its soaring stained glass windows, which become gradually lighter approaching the altar to symbolize coming closer to God's light. Designer Harold Wagoner took cues from the aerospace world, including the winglike tetrahedrons of the walls and the propeller-inspired pews. Air Force Academy Cadet Chapel.

Catholic sanctuary has a basilica plan and seats 500; the Jewish sanctuary is circular in shape and seats 100; and the largest is the 1,200-seat Protestant sanctuary, where a 47-foot tall aluminum cross, symbolizing a bird in flight, is suspended over the altar.

An equally dramatic building is the Chapel of the Holy Cross (1956), located about three miles from Sedona, Arizona, and 150 feet above the floor of the Verde River Valley. The chapel rises from an outcropping of red sandstone at the base of a 1,500-foot vertical cliff. Its reinforced concrete shell is 12 inches thick. Two ends of the chapel have smoked glass windows that permit a clear view of the magnificent scenery behind the altar.

The Chapel of the Holy Cross does not try to blend into its environment; rather, like a Gothic cathedral that stands in contrast to its surrounding buildings, the geometric form of the chapel makes it stand out among all the organic forms of the landscape around it.
Chapel of the Holy Cross (1956), Sedona, Arizona.

CHAPTER 7

PACIFIC REGION

Roman Catholic, Russian Orthodox, New England Protestants—each group that settled in the Pacific region came with its missionaries and its own particular style of church architecture. Material, funds, and technology determined how each style was going to be reinterpreted in a new, often alien environment.

OPPOSITE: **The altar at La Purisima Concepcion has been restored to its pristine Spanish colonial state. Father Mariano Payéras, onetime president of the California Missions, is interred beneath it.** La Purisima Concepcion (1815–18), near Lompoc, California.

THE MISSIONS

The first to arrive in California, Spanish missionaries began to construct a chain of missions along El Camino Real in 1770. Alta California, as the area was then known, became part of the United States after the Mexican-American War in 1848; its cultural character was changed when gold was discovered.

San Diego was the site of the first mission in this region—San Diego de Alcala (1769), which was founded by Spanish Franciscan priest Junipero Serra. Twenty missions soon followed, concluding with San Francisco Solano (1823). Founded in 1787, La Purisima Concepcion near Lompoc was the eleventh. The mission's first buildings were hastily constructed and were replaced by more permanent structures in 1802; these were then destroyed in 1812 by a devastating earthquake and flood. Undeterred, the priests and the Chumash Indians reconstructed the mission on a safer site about four miles away. The four-foot-thick walls of the new buildings were considered virtually earthquake proof, but this did not prevent the mission from going into ruin in the mid-19th century after it was secularized and sold.

The Civilian Conservation Corps began reconstruction on La Purisima Concepcion in 1935 using the same methods as its original builders. Laid out in a linear fashion, the mission consists of a walled cemetery that adjoins the church, military

LEFT: **The eleventh Spanish Franciscan mission in Alta California, La Purisima Concepcion was the center of a community of more than 1,000 Chumash Indians in the late 18th century. After falling into a state of neglect for nearly a century, the site was meticulously restored as a state historic park.** La Purisima Concepcion.

Restored for the first time in 1921—nearly a century after the founding of the Wai'oli mission—"The Green Church" is a Hanalei landmark. The congregation to this day sings missionary-translated hymns in Hawaiian. Old Wai'oli Hui'ia Church (1832), Hanalei, Kauai.

quarters, workshops, and priests' quarters. The distinguishing feature on the exterior is a three-bell *campanario.* The interior has been restored to its original appearance, including chancel walls painted to appear as marble alternating with panels filled with floral motifs. Behind and above the altar are small niches that hold images of saints flanking a statue of the Virgin set in a larger semidomed niche.

The first Russians to enter Alaska in 1741 were not in search of land to conquer or souls to save; rather, they were seeking fur, particularly otter and seal. The missionaries sent to the region by the Russian Orthodox Church did not receive a warm welcome from the fur trappers or the region's native people. This did not dissuade them from settling on the Kodiak Archipelago, where in 1794 they erected the first Russian Orthodox Church on the continent.

While that church no longer exists, St. Michael's Cathedral in Sitka, Alaska, still stands. Reconstructed in 1976 after a fire, the cathedral was originally built in 1848 by Bishop Veniaminov. Unlike most

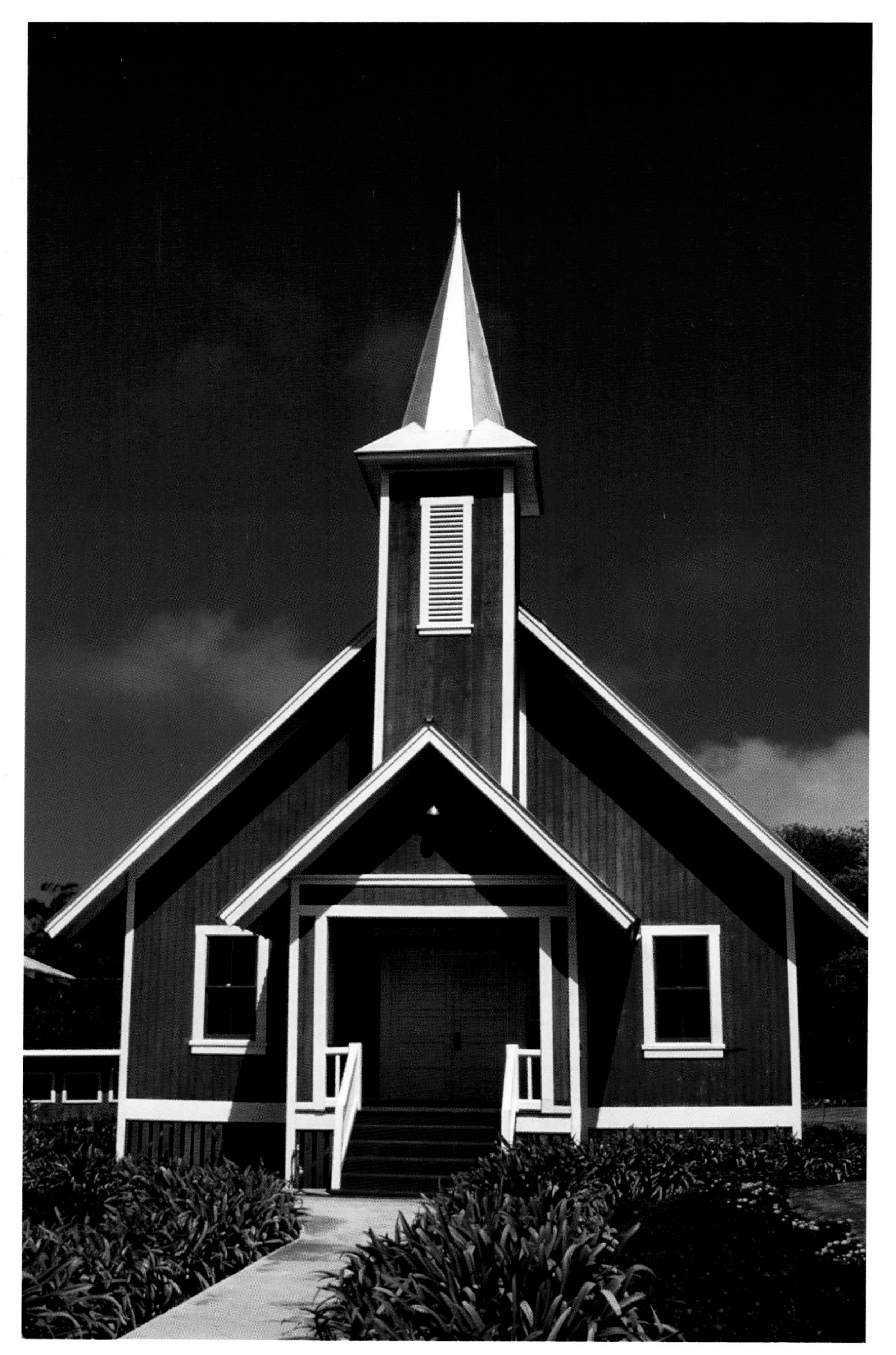

ICONOSTASIS AND ICONS

All Orthodox churches have a platform that supports an iconostasis. Some close off the sanctuary housing of the altar completely, while others are pierced to allow worshipers a glimpse of what is happening behind the screen. In the center of the iconostasis are the Royal Doors, behind which stands the altar table. It is here that the priest performs the sacred rites prior to bringing the consecrated host out through the Royal Doors to present to the congregation. The icons hanging on the iconostasis are generally arranged in the following fashion: the icons of the four evangelists and, in some instances, the Annunciation are on the Royal Doors; the icon of the Last Supper appears above the doors; and the side doors, called Deacon's Doors, have icons of angels and other holy people. Facing the iconostasis, to the immediate left of the Royal Doors, is the icon of *Theotokos,* the Virgin Mary and the Christ Child. To the immediate right of the Royal Doors is the icon of the Glorified Christ. Large iconostases will have additional rows of icons, usually of apostles, prophets, and the holy figure for whom the church is named. Regardless of its size, the iconostasis is always crowned with a cross.

Russian Orthodox Churches, St. Michael's has a cruciform plan. The building is entered through a large tower capped with a small spire; a large dome topped by a lantern supporting a small onion dome covers the nave. As in all Orthodox churches, an iconostasis encloses the altar in the sanctuary.

When the first Congregational missionaries arrived in Hawaii in 1820, the islands were in the midst of turmoil following the death of King Kamehameha. His son, Liholiho, who had been exposed to Western culture, had lessened the power of the priests and subsequently the native religion. This prepared the way for the missionaries, who found the islands a "fruitful field" where they could sow the seeds of Christianity. Initially, the missionaries built simple thatched huts to hold services. These were later replaced by more permanent structures, such as Old Wai'oli Hui'ia Church on the island of Kauai. Built in 1832, the church has been reconstructed several times but retains its original character. It is a timber building with an open four-sided *lanai,* or porch. The original tall hipped roof was thatch but is now shingled.

Alaska is home to many descendants of the Russians who settled the land before it was sold to the United States in 1867. Rebuilt after the original cathedral burned to the ground in 1966, St. Michael's is a testament to this heritage. St. Michael's Cathedral (1848, 1976), Sitka, Alaska.

FAR RIGHT: **Originally named the Zion Lutheran Church, this Gothic Revival church is next to one of the oldest cemeteries in Washington. The architecture borrows largely from Scandinavian influences, not the more Gothic-style designs favored in Episcopal churches.** The Little White Church on the Hill (1890), near Silvana, Washington.

MINERS, PIONEERS, AND ENTREPRENEURS

The natural resources found throughout the Pacific region attracted adventurers looking for instant wealth, immigrants searching for tillable land, and entrepreneurs seeking new opportunities. The effort it took to mine the gold, till the soil, and establish new businesses did not leave a lot of time to think about religion. But this did not deter the circuit-riding preachers who were intent on saving the souls of those engaged in material pursuits. Mexican miners founded Sonora, California, and named the city after their hometown. Yankee entrepreneurs transformed it into one of the largest and wealthiest towns in California's "mother lode" country.

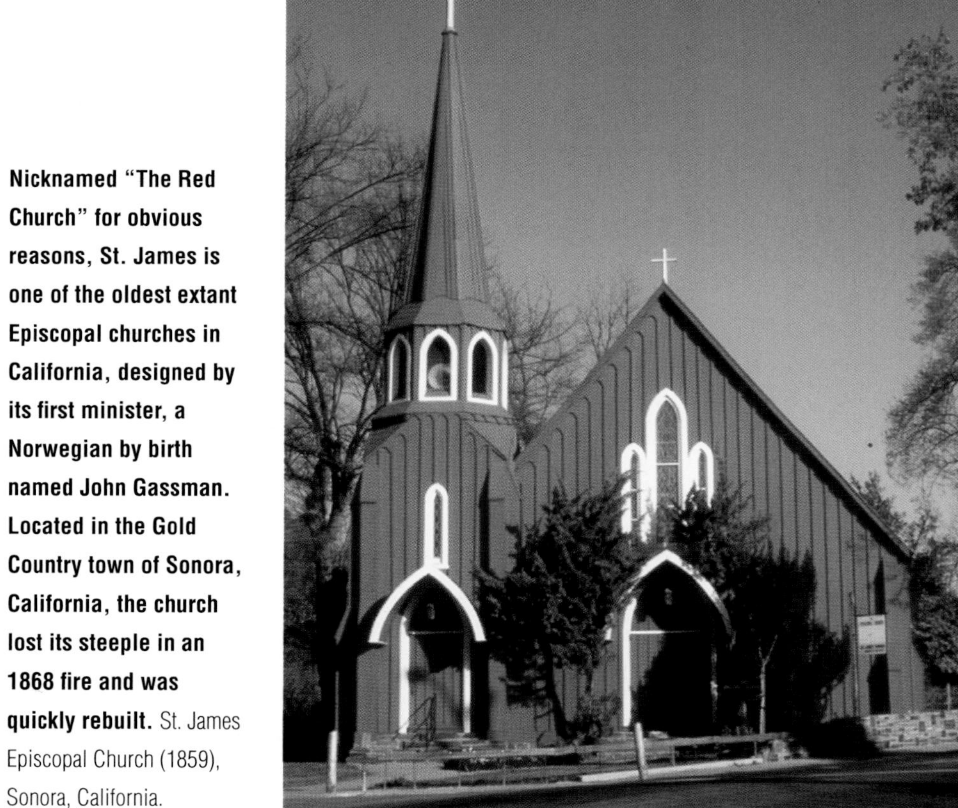

Nicknamed "The Red Church" for obvious reasons, St. James is one of the oldest extant Episcopal churches in California, designed by its first minister, a Norwegian by birth named John Gassman. Located in the Gold Country town of Sonora, California, the church lost its steeple in an 1868 fire and was quickly rebuilt. St. James Episcopal Church (1859), Sonora, California.

In 1857, San Francisco's Episcopal bishop sent one of his priests to Sonora to organize a congregation and oversee the erection of a church. Two years later St. James Episcopal Church (1859) was constructed. The church's appearance leaves no doubt as to its source—Richard Upjohn's ubiquitous book, *Rural Architecture.* It is a typical Carpenter Gothic Revival structure with vertical board-and-batten siding, pointed arched windows, and an impressive bell tower and spire. St. James is one of the oldest extant Episcopal churches in California.

Home to the longest continuously operating sawmill in the country until it ceased production in 1995, the logging town of Port Gamble, Washington, was founded by transplants from Maine. A house of worship in the founders' hometown inspired the design of this church. St. Paul's Episcopal Church (1870), Port Gamble, Washington.

The Gothic Revival style was gaining popularity at the time this region was being settled, so it is not surprising that many of the rural churches built here in the 19th century exhibit Gothic Revival traits. These small wooden churches were inexpensive and easy to build, especially in areas where lumber was readily available.

Scandinavians, most of them Lutheran, began to arrive in Washington in great numbers in the 1880s. Some came to farm, while others found jobs as lumberjacks. The Little White Church on the Hill (1890) near Silvana is typical of the churches they erected. Although Gothic Revival in style, it differs from the Carpenter Gothic favored by Episcopalians. Instead, this small church exhibits characteristics of the small rural churches found in Scandinavia. The main difference is that rather than being built of stone covered with stucco, the structure is clad in horizontal clapboard painted white. Its three-part division visible on the exterior—narthex, nave, and chancel—along with the tower and spire placed on the narthex's roof reveal its ancestry.

Some settlers chose not to be fashionable; instead they selected styles that were either familiar to them or had a special symbolic meaning. Families from East Machias, Maine, founded Port Gamble, Washington, a company mill town, in 1853. They erected a congregational church in 1870 that is modeled after the First Congregational Church in their hometown. Originally congregational,

Built by Portuguese settlers and inspired by the shape of their native country's royal crown, this church is the only octagonal building in the entire state of Hawaii. The structure was completely restored in 1992. Holy Ghost Roman Catholic Church (1894–97), Kula, Maui.

the church is now St. Paul's Episcopal Church. With its arched windows, fine carved details, and beautiful entrance tower and spire, the white clapboard church is reminiscent of Georgian-style churches erected in the colonies prior to the Revolutionary War.

More unusual is the church built by indentured Portuguese immigrants who came to work on the sugar plantations on the island of Maui, Hawaii. Following fulfillment of their contracts, many chose to stay and homestead on the island. By 1882 the community grew large enough to require a priest, and by 1894, it could afford to build a church. According to tradition, the unusual plan of Holy Ghost Roman Catholic Church (1894–97) is due to its model—a crown of 13th-century Queen Elizabeth (Isabella) of Portugal. A replica of the crown is housed in the church and plays an important role in the Portuguese community's Holy Ghost celebration. The church has been recently restored.

NEW BEGINNINGS: THE MODERN ERA

The Romantic Movement and its interest in revival styles remained fashionable in this region well into the 20th century. Architects continued to look to the past for inspiration, but some of the more creative ones added their own personal interpretation of it. One of the more imaginative was Bernard Maybeck (1862–1957), who studied at L'école des Beaux-Arts in Paris before returning to Berkeley, California, where he spent his entire career. Maybeck borrowed from a variety of styles for his most admired work, the wonderfully exotic and eclectic First Church of Christ, Scientist (1910) in Berkeley.

Like Frank Lloyd Wright's Unity Temple in Oak Park, Illinois, First Church of Christ, Scientist is made of concrete, wood, and steel. The building's horizontal profile on the exterior is remindful of Wright's Prairie style, but its low-pitched gable roofs with their broad overhanging eaves originally clad in sheet metal appear to have been borrowed from a Japanese pagoda. The church interior's Greek Cross plan, centered on a large square central auditorium, is characteristic of Byzantine architecture.

Californians began to explore their state's Spanish heritage in the first decades of the 20th century. Spurring this interest was the 1915 San Diego Exposition, which featured Bertram G. Goodhue's Spanish-influenced design for the Exposition's California building. What is unusual is that unlike in Texas and Arizona, the Spanish never erected buildings in the elaborate Baroque style in California. But this fact didn't stop Albert C. Martin from designing the monumental St. Vincent de Paul Roman Catholic Church (1923–25) in this fashion. Located in Los Angeles, California, the cruciform basilica-plan church features an elaborately decorated façade and single multitiered bell tower; a large dome on the exterior with colorful tiles hovers over the crossing.

One of the crowning achievements of a great career, Bernard Maybeck's First Church of Christ, Scientist in Berkeley incorporates materials traditionally regarded as industrial—concrete, cement tile, and factory windows—into a design renowned for its eclecticism and interplay of space and light. First Church of Christ, Scientist (1910), Berkeley, California.

While the Spanish missions in California aren't built in the Spanish Baroque style of their counterparts in the Southeast, Albert C. Martin designed a fine specimen of the style in 20th-century Los Angeles. The detailed façade was sculpted out of Indiana limestone. St. Vincent de Paul Roman Catholic Church (1923–25), Los Angeles, California.

FAR RIGHT: **Pietro Belluschi, onetime architecture dean at Massachusetts Institute of Technology, designed this strikingly modern San Francisco landmark. Atop the 190-foot geometric cupola, defined by bold lines curving elegantly skyward, is a 55-foot cross; below it are earthquake-proof pylons drilled 90 feet into the bedrock.** St. Mary's Cathedral (1967–70), San Francisco, California.

THE MODERN ERA

In the years following World War II, California began to attract large numbers of people seeking a warmer climate and employment in the state's expanding industries. As the cities grew, so too, did the need for additional houses of worship—buildings that would express the region's forward-looking ideology. But people also needed quiet contemplative spaces where they could escape the cacophony of the cities and the roar of the highways. John Lloyd Wright, son of Frank Lloyd Wright, designed one such place.

Followers of the 18th-century theologian Emanuel Swedenborg (1688–1772) invited John Lloyd Wright to design a worship space that would be in harmony with its beautiful natural setting. Wayfarer's Chapel (1949–51) in a secluded location near Palos Verdes, California, has been described as a "natural church." All that is visible from the road approaching the site is a tall, thin angular stone and concrete tower that appears to be rising up from the vegetation. Set originally in the midst of coastal redwoods that have since been replaced by other trees, the church is almost entirely made of transparent glass. The structure's roof design emulates the trees that surround it. The result is a quiet, peaceful space that invites contemplation.

On a far larger scale is the highly visible St. Mary's Cathedral (1967–70) in San Francisco, designed by one

John Lloyd Wright, the son of Frank Lloyd Wright, was a great architect on his own merit. Beyond his design for the nearby Hollywood Bowl, Wayfarer's Chapel, long a favorite wedding spot for Hollywood celebrities, blends seamlessly into its natural surroundings. Wayfarer's Chapel (1949–51), near Palos Verdes, California.

The stark yet bold interior of St. Mary's Cathedral is dominated by marble, stained glass, and an enormous kinetic sculpture that rises to the apex of the cupola. St. Mary's Cathedral.

of the most innovative architects of the postwar era, civil engineer and architect Pietro Belluschi (1899–1994). It is the first cathedral in the United States designed specifically to meet the liturgical demands of Vatican II. Standing in the midst of a plaza on the crest of a hill and sheathed in white Italian travertine, the cathedral is a striking presence in the city. Referred to by detractors as "the Bendix" for its distinctive shape that to some resembles a washing-machine agitator, the cathedral's basic geometrical form is four hyperbolic paraboloids of precast concrete that soar upward, twisting as they rise and intersecting at right angles. The nave, sanctuary, transepts, baptistery, and narthex are all united in one large column-free 200-foot square interior. Suspended above the altar is a *baldacchino,* created by Richard Lippold, made of thin silver and gold cylinders.

Cars and people come together in the Garden Grove Church (The Crystal Cathedral) (1978–80), designed by Philip Johnson and John Burgee at the behest of Reverend Robert Schuller, the congregation's popular preacher (see pages 124 and 24–25). Larger than Notre Dame in Paris and considered the first of the "megachurches," it seats 3,000 people. The steel-and-glass structure's plan is basically a four-pointed star that reaches up to 128 feet at its apex. To accommodate large gatherings, portions of the exterior walls open to allow congregants seated in their cars to participate in the worship service.

Everything is big inside Dr. Robert Schuller's Crystal Cathedral, from the seating capacity (about 3,000) to the big-screen television to the right of the altar to the organs (around 16,000 pipes in all). Garden Grove Church (The Crystal Cathedral) (1978–80), Garden Grove, California.

POSTMODERN

In the postmodern era, architects once again began to quote from the past while making changes to the vocabulary in order to speak to present-day worshipers. One example is St. Gregory of Nyssa Episcopal Church (1994–95) in San Francisco. The structure's unusual plan accommodates the congregation's liturgy, which is divided into two sections: Liturgy of the Word, which includes Bible readings, and Liturgy of the Eucharist, or Holy Communion.

The church is named after an early Christian bishop, Gregory of Nyssa from Cappadocia (now in modern

FAR RIGHT: **The murals bedecking the walls of St. Gregory's reflect the style of its namesake's homeland of Cappadocia, an area that is now within Turkey's boundaries. Among the pictured saints is St. Gregory himself.** St. Gregory of Nyssa Episcopal Church (1994–95), San Francisco, California.

Turkey), who is described as a mystic, theologian, and humanist. The design of the church reflects its namesake's Eastern heritage, although the first impression from the exterior is that it belongs to the tradition of California architecture best expressed by Maybeck in his design of the First Church of Christ, Scientist in Berkeley. Like Maybeck, the architects have borrowed from several historic styles, mainly from the Orthodox tradition. The use of wood shingles throughout and the bell tower on the gabled Liturgy of the Word section are remindful of rural church architecture in Russia. The octagonal plan of the Liturgy of the Eucharist section, which is covered by a 60-foot-high cupola, looks back to Byzantine designs favored by Orthodox Christians. The antiphonal seating (rows of seats facing each other, separated by a central aisle) found in the Liturgy of the Word section originated in medieval synagogues built by Sephardic Jews in Spain. Much of the church's decoration is in the Orthodox tradition, including icons (but not an iconostasis), wall paintings, and mosaics.

Our Lady of the Angels is a foot longer than St. Patrick's Cathedral in New York City. The contemporary $195 million building is the newest Roman Catholic cathedral in the western United States. Cathedral of Our Lady of the Angels (1998–2002), Los Angeles, California.

Long anticipated and rife with controversy is the Cathedral of Our Lady of the Angels (1998–2002) in Los Angeles, designed by Spanish architect Jose Rafael Moneo. This monumental church represents the attempt by one architect and his patron, Cardinal Mahoney, to combine elements from the past with the modern need for a "megachurch" that will fulfill the psalmist's request that we worship the Lord in the beauty of holiness.

Best viewed, perhaps appropriately, from a freeway, the cathedral has been called by some detractors the "yellow armadillo." From a distance its adobe-colored concrete panels appear to be similar to the scales found on an armadillo, but its color is supposed to be reminiscent of the city's Hispanic heritage, as is its traditional *campanario.* The cathedral is entered by first walking through a large open plaza that leads to the façade; the main entry off to one side is distinguished by enormous bronze doors designed by Robert Graham.

PHOTO CREDITS

Front cover: Pat & Chuck Blackley

Back cover: **Michael P. Gadomski** (left); **Kay Shaw Photography** (right); **Courtesy of St. Therese Wilson, North Carolina** (center).

Pat & Chuck Blackley: Title page, 5, 10, 36, 39, 40, 54, 113; **Courtesy of Chapel of St. Basil, Houston, Texas:** 99; **Courtesy of Church of Our Saviour, Luka, Mississippi:** 91; **Eliot Cohen:** 22, 43 (left), 107; **Bruce Coleman, Inc.:** Kate McDonald: 116; Wendell Metzen: 67; © **Corbis:** Tony Arruza: 47; Bettmann: 30–31; Philip James Corwin: 24–25; Richard Cummins: 79; Kevin Fleming: Endsheets, 15–16, 42 (top), 94; Todd Gipstein: 41; Robert Holmes: 21, 124 (top); Wolfgang Kaehler: 118 (top); Andy Keate; 12, Layne Kennedy: 70; Robert Landau: 125; Francis G. Mayer: 50 (top right & bottom right); Buddy Mays: 14; John McAnulty: 72; MIT Collection: 11, 82 (top); Kevin R. Morris: 105, 106; G.E. Kidder Smith: 8 (bottom), 58 (bottom), 60; Lee Snider: 45 (top), 55 (bottom), 57, 77; Peter M. Wilson: 104 (bottom); **Courtesy of Dickeyville Grotto, Dickeyville, Wisconsin:** 81; **E. David Luria Photography:** 59, 64; **Courtesy of First Christian Church, Columbus, Indiana:** 32, 83; **Michael P. Gadomski:** 53, 119; **Mark E. Gibson/Gibson Stock Photography:** 86, 103 (bottom); **Courtesy of Scott arp/therestorationmovement.com:** 55 (top); **Courtesy of Holy Family Catholic Church, Caholia, Illinois:** 69; **Courtesy of Hillsman Stuart Jackson/Southern Methodist University:** 95; **Kay Shaw Photography:** Contents, 28, 120; **Courtesy of Kingston United Methodist, Mississippi:** 90; **James Kirkikis:** 33, 37, 38, 44, 46 (right), 48 (top); **Carol Kitman:** 87, 103 (top); **Elliot H. Koeppel:** 118 (bottom); **Kathy J. Kunce:** 100–101, 109 (bottom); **Library of Congress:** 20, 29, 42 (bottom), 45 (bottom), 56, 71, 73 (bottom left); **Courtesy of Alan Oakes/UCLA University Catholic Center:** 93; **Doug Ohman/Pioneer Photography:** 75; **Courtesy of Oklahoma State Historical Society:** 88; **Jack Olson:** 76 (bottom left), 110 (bottom); **Chuck Place:** 102, 114; **Carl Purcell:** 46 (left); **James P. Rowan:** 9, 76 (top right), 78 (top left & bottom), 80, 82 (bottom); **Skjold Photographs:** 62; **G.E. Kidder Smith, Courtesy of Kidder Smith Collection, Rotch Visual Collections, M.I.T.:** 50 (bottom left); **Lee Snider/Photo Images:** 8 (top), 13, 43 (right), 48 (bottom), 52, 58 (top), 65, 68, 84–85; **Courtesy of St. Gregory of Nyssa Episcopal Church, San Francisco, California:** 124 (bottom); **Courtesy of St. Mary's Episcopal Church, Green Cove Springs, Florida:** 61; **Courtesy of St. Therese Wilson, North Carolina:** 34; **Courtesy of St. Thomas More Catholic Church, Paducah, Kentucky:** 97, 98; **Gina Summers:** 35; **SuperStock:** 89, 121 (bottom); Ping Amranand: 63; Tom Benoit: 122 (top); Tom Brakefield: 115; Michele Burgess: 96 (bottom), 110 (top); Color Image, Inc.: 112 (top); Richard Cummins: 104 (top), 111, 112 (bottom), 123; Steven Dahlman: 78 (top right); Dale Jorgensen: 122 (bottom); Luther Linkhart: 108; Ernest Manewal: 117; Lynn Radeka: 109 (top); Steve Vidler: 6–7; **Terry Wild Studio:** 49; **Courtesy of Third Reformed Church, Holland, Michigan:** 74; **Trinity Church, Boston:** 66; **Courtesy of Tuskegee Institute:** 96 (top); **Unicorn Stock Photos:** Tommy Dodson: 121 (top); Jean Higgins: 92; H. Schmeiser: 51; **Steve Warble:** 73 (top right); **Courtesy of Wesley United Methodist Church, Minneapolis, Minnesota:** 23.